the life-changing
magic of NOT GIVING A F*CK

# the life-changing
# magic of NOT GIVING A F*CK

how to stop spending time you don't have
with people you don't like
doing things you don't want to do

## sarah knight

Little, Brown and Company
*New York   Boston   London*

Little, Brown and Company
Hachette Book Group
1290 Avenue of the Americas, New York, NY 10104
littlebrown.com

First Edition: December 2015

Little, Brown and Company is a division of Hachette Book Group, Inc. The Little, Brown name and logo are trademarks of Hachette Book Group, Inc.

The publisher is not responsible for websites (or their content) that are not owned by the publisher.

The Hachette Speakers Bureau provides a wide range of authors for speaking events. To find out more, go to hachettespeakersbureau.com or call (866) 376-6591.

Illustrations and hand-lettering by Lauren Harms

ISBN 978-0-316-27072-4
LCCN 2015952380

10 9 8 7 6 5 4 3 2 1

RRD-C

Printed in the United States of America

# A fucking disclaimer

This is a book about not giving a fuck. In order to practically quantify my methods, I've confessed to banishing many objects, concepts, events, activities, and people from my life. You may not agree with all of my choices. Fair. You may even think you recognize yourself in these pages — particularly if you are a parent of small children, a karaoke enthusiast, a friend, family member, or former colleague of mine. If so, you're either correct, or delusional. In any case, if you're offended by anything I've written, then you **really** need this book. Proceed immediately to page 25: "You Need to Stop Giving a Fuck About What Other People Think."

Also note: There's no fucking way this parody was prepared, approved, endorsed, or authorized by Marie Kondo or her publishers.

# Contents

# Deciding not to give a fuck   43

# Not giving a fuck  **123**

# IV

# The magic of not giving a fuck dramatically transforms your life  **171**

the life-changing
magic of **NOT GIVING A F\*CK**

# Introduction

If you're like me, you've been giving too many fucks about too many things for too long. You're overextended and overburdened by life. Stressed out, anxious, maybe even panic-stricken about your commitments.

*The Life-Changing Magic of Not Giving a Fuck* is for all of us who work too much, play too little, and never have enough time to devote to the people and things that truly make us happy.

I was almost thirty years old when I began to realize it was possible to stop giving so many fucks, but I was nearly forty before I figured out how to make it happen on a grand scale. This book is a culmination of everything I've learned about not giving a fuck, a testament to the pleasure it has brought me, and a step-by-step guide for those wishing to free themselves from the shackles of fuck-giving in pursuit of healthier, happier lives.

If the title sounds familiar, congratulations! You haven't

been living under a rock as *The Life-Changing Magic of Tidying Up* by Japanese decluttering expert Marie Kondo has climbed bestseller lists all over the world. Millions of people have discovered her two-step KonMari Method, discarding items that do not "spark joy" and then organizing the ones they have left. The result is a clean, tranquil living space that, Ms. Kondo claims, promotes transformation even outside the home.

**So what does a Japanese book about tidying up have to do with my manifesto on not giving a fuck?**

Why, I thought you'd never ask!

As prim, genteel, and effective at organizing your physical clutter as Ms. Kondo is, I've got something else in store for you...


## Tidying up your fuck drawer

In the summer of 2015 I quit my job at a major publishing house, a career that had been fifteen years in the making, to start my own business as a freelance editor and writer. The day I walked out of my high-rise office building — sliding down that corporate ladder faster than a stripper down the last pole of the night — I eliminated a whole category of fucks I had previously given to supervisors, coworkers, my commute, my wardrobe, my alarm clock, and more.

I stopped giving a fuck about Sales Conference. I

stopped giving a fuck about "business-casual" and "town-hall meetings." I stopped keeping track of my vacation days like a prisoner tallying her sentence in hash marks on the cell-block wall.

Once I was released from the yoke of corporate ennui, I naturally had a bit of time on my hands and the freedom to spend it as I wished. I slept until I was damn well ready to get up, ate lunch with my husband, worked on a freelance gig or two (or maybe went to the beach), and avoided the New York City subway as much as humanly possible.

I also read *The Life-Changing Magic of Tidying Up*. As a generally tidy person, I didn't think I was in dire need of Ms. Kondo's advice, but I'm always looking for ways to make my apartment look more like *Real Simple* magazine — and, hey, my time was my own to work, nap, or declutter as I saw fit.

Well, let me tell you, this little book works as advertised. It was almost...dare I say...*magic*?

Within hours, I had KonMari'd my husband's sock drawer, which involves getting rid of socks you don't like and never wear (or, in this case, socks I knew *he* didn't like and never wore), then refolding the rest to look like little soldiers standing at attention, so when you next open the drawer, you can see all of them in one glance. After viewing the results, my husband — who'd initially thought I was batshit crazy to spend my time organizing his sock drawer — was a convert. He did the rest of his drawers and his closet all by himself the very next day.

If you haven't read Marie Kondo's book, allow me to explain why we were so motivated to do this work.

Beyond discarding items of clothing we no longer need or enjoy (and therefore being excited about all of our remaining options), we've decreased the time spent figuring out what to wear (because we can see everything in a single drawer with one look), nothing gets "lost" in a drawer anymore (because we follow Ms. Kondo's method of stand-up folding), and we do a lot less laundry (because we haven't tricked ourselves into thinking we're "out" of clothes when in fact the good stuff was just crumpled up in the back of the bureau under the pants that don't fit).

In other words: Life is significantly better now that we can see all of our socks. And I ran around for weeks evangelizing to anybody who would listen (and many who would not).

Suddenly, with all the job-quitting and sock-tidying, I found myself in a life-changing kind of mood!

As I contemplated my exceptionally tidy home, I felt more peaceful, sure. I like a clear surface and a well-organized kitchen cabinet. But it was the freedom I felt from leaving a job I wasn't happy in — and being able to add people and things and events and hobbies that made me happy *back* into my life — that truly sparked joy. These were things that had been displaced not by twenty-two pairs of balled-up socks, but by **too many obligations and too much *mental* clutter.**

That's when I realized . . . it's not really about the socks, is it?

Don't get me wrong, I admire Marie Kondo for starting a revolution of decluttering physical spaces to bring more joy to one's life. It worked on me, and it's clearly working on millions of people around the world. But as she says in her book, "Life truly begins after you have put your house in order."

**Well, I put my house in order. The real magic happened when I focused on my fucks.**

Let's back up a little bit.

## The art of mental decluttering

I was a born fuck-giver. Maybe you are too.

As a self-described overachieving perfectionist, I gave my fucks liberally all throughout my childhood and adolescence. I tackled numerous projects, tasks, and standardized tests in order to prove myself worthy of respect and admiration from my family, friends, and even casual acquaintances. I socialized with people I did not like in order to appear benevolent; I performed jobs that were beneath me in order to appear helpful; I ate things that disgusted me in order to appear gracious. In short, I gave way too many fucks for far, far too long.

This was no way to live.

The first time I met someone who just didn't give a fuck was in my early twenties. We'll call him Jeff. A successful business owner with a large circle of friends, Jeff simply could not be bothered to do things he didn't want to do. And yet, he was widely liked and respected. He didn't show up to your toddler's dance recital or to watch you cross the finish line at your seventeenth 5K, but it was okay, because that was just him, you know? He was a perfectly nice, sociable, and well-thought-of guy, but he clearly reserved his fucks for things that were especially important to him — having a close relationship with his kids, playing golf, catching *Jeopardy!* every night. The rest of it?

**Could. Not. Give. A. Fuck.**

And he always seemed so positively self-satisfied and, well, happy.

*Huh,* I often thought to myself after spending time with him. *I wish I could be more like Jeff.*

Later, in my midtwenties, I had a downstairs neighbor who was an absolute nightmare. But for some reason I cared enough about his opinion of me to submit to his insane requests (like the time he corralled a friend to stomp around my apartment in high-heeled boots while I *listened* with him from his living room below, hearing nothing, but gamely agreeing that it was "a little noisy").

He was clearly unhinged — so why did it matter if he liked me or not? In retrospect, I should have stopped giving a fuck about Mr. Rosenberg the first time he accused my roommate of "heavy exercising" in the bedroom above his... when my roommate had been traveling in Europe for two weeks.

Then, nearing thirty, I got engaged and started

planning a wedding — an act that demands a veritable cornucopia of fucks given: the budget, the venue, the catering, the dress, the photos, the flowers, the band, the guest list, the invitations (wording and thickness thereof), the vows, the cake, and everything else — the list goes on. Many of these things I truly cared about, but some of them I didn't; and yet, I gave each and every one of them a fuck because I didn't know any better. I became so stressed out that **I was about as far from self-satisfied and happy as it gets.** By the time the Big Day rolled around, I had migraines, a persistent stomachache, and a case of hives the same rosy pink as the floral detail on my gown.

Looking back, was arguing with my husband over playing "Brown-Eyed Girl" at the reception really worth my time (or his)?

Had minute attention to detail re: the selection of passed hors d'oeuvres really been necessary when I didn't get to eat any of them because they were passed during our photos?

Nope.

But — and here's where the tide turned ever so slightly — I had won one small victory: I may have had to give a fuck about the guest list (because I *definitely* gave a fuck about the budget), but you know what I never gave a fuck about? Seating charts!

In deciding that all of my wedding guests were grown-ass adults who didn't need my help in choosing a seat for the privilege of being fed, soused, and entertained on my dime, I had eliminated hours — perhaps a dozen or more —

of poring over the event-space schematics and moving aunts, uncles, and plus-ones around like beads on a goddamn abacus. Win!

After the wedding fuckscapade, I was exhausted. I'd been pushed to my breaking point. Yet I'd also seen a silver lining in that abandoned seating chart. I knew that seating charts were *supposed* to matter to me, but they didn't. Instead of putting that feeling of obligation ahead of my own personal preference, I'd just decided not to give a fuck and let the butts land where they may. And did anyone complain to the blushing bride? No, they did not.

*Hmm…*

Little by little over the next several years, **I stopped giving a fuck about small things that annoyed me.** I RSVP'd "no" to a couple of after-work mixers. I unfriended some truly irritating people on Facebook. I refused to suffer through another "reading" of your "play."

And little by little, I started feeling better. Less burdened. More peaceful. I hung up on telemarketers; I said no to a weekend trip with toddlers; I stopped watching season 2 of *True Detective* after only one episode. I was becoming my true self, able to focus more on people and things that actually, as Marie Kondo might say, sparked joy.

Soon, I realized I had my own insights to share with regard to life-changing magic.

Brings you joy? Then by all means, keep giving a fuck.

But perhaps the more pertinent question is:

**Does it annoy?**

If so, you need to stop giving a fuck, posthaste. And I can show you how.

I've developed a program for **decluttering and reorganizing your *mental* space by not giving a fuck**, wherein *not giving a fuck* means not spending time, energy, and/or money on things that neither make you happy nor improve your life (annoy), so that you have *more* time, energy, and/or money to devote to the things that do (bring joy).

I call it the NotSorry Method. It has two steps:

1. Deciding what you don't give a fuck about

2. Not giving a fuck about those things

And of course, "Not Sorry" is how you should feel when you've accomplished this.

My method is quite simple — and this book offers you the tools and perspective to master it, and to radically improve your day-to-day existence. **In fact, once you begin implementing NotSorry, you'll never want or need to give an extraneous fuck ever again.**

## The magic of not giving a fuck

In this book, you will learn:

- Why giving a fuck about what other people think is your worst enemy — and how to stop doing it

- How to sort your fucks into categories for ease in identifying annoy vs. joy

- Simple criteria for whether or not you should give a fuck (e.g., "Does this affect anyone other than me?")

- The keys to not giving a fuck *without* being an asshole

- The importance of making (and sticking to) a Fuck Budget

- How mastering the art of giving fewer, better fucks can transform your life

- And much, much more!

Just think about how much better your life would be if you could say no to things you really don't give a fuck about and have more time, energy, and money to say yes to the things you do.

For example, when I stopped giving a fuck about putting on makeup before leaving my apartment just to go to the grocery store, I gained ten leisurely minutes to sit on my couch and read the *Us Weekly* I'd just bought at said grocery store.

Or, when I stopped giving a fuck about going to baby showers — an activity I positively *loathe* — I gained untold Sunday afternoons of freedom!

And all that time I save by not going to baby showers?

Well, first, I pour myself a double shot of Patrón, and then it's only a few clicks on Giggle.com to order a shiny new breast pump for the mother-to-be, after which I raise a glass to my college roommate's Cabo Wabo Spring Break '98 wet T-shirt contest–winning boobs.

Fare thee well, ladies!

Ten minutes online versus four hours of diaper-decorating games and virgin punch? For me, it's a no-brainer. For you, baby showers could be a fuck-worthy activity, while it's, I don't know, prowling yard sales every weekend with your deal-seeking significant other that brings you no end of annoy.

The specifics don't matter. What matters is, if you follow my NotSorry Method for not giving a fuck, your spirit will be lighter, your calendar will be clearer, and your time and energy will be spent on only the things and people you enjoy.

**It's life-changing. Swear to God.**

# 1

# On giving, and not giving, a fuck

Ask yourself the following question: *Am I stressed out, overbooked, and/or underwhelmed by life?*

If the answer is yes to any of these, then pause for a moment to ask yourself: *Why?*

I'm willing to bet the answer is: Because you give too many fucks. Or, more specifically, because you *think you have to* give those fucks.

I'm here to help.

During the course of this book, you'll see the term *giving a fuck* used in two ways:

- There's the colloquial sense of caring about something, which factors into Step 1 (deciding what you don't give a fuck about).

- Then there's a literal sense of actually giving a fuck *to* someone or something, in the form of time, energy, and/or money. This factors into Step 2 (not giving a fuck about those things).

In both senses, the only way to change your life for the better is to stop giving *so fucking many of them.* My NotSorry Method minimizes the time, energy, and money you spend on useless people and things. Admit it: you know exactly who and what I'm talking about!

It doesn't have to be this way. Let's get started, shall we?

# Why should I give a fuck?

This is one of life's essential questions. Or at least it should be.

Rather than blindly pressing forward and saying *Yes, YES, **YES!!!*** to all of the people and things that demand your time, energy, and/or money (including purchasing and reading this book), the first thing you should be asking yourself before uttering that dirty little three-letter word is, *Do I really give a fuck?*

You may not realize it, but the number of fucks you personally have to give is a finite and precious commodity. Give too many, and you run out — it's like getting to zero in your bank account — which results in your feeling anxious, stressed out, and desperate. That's no good! Later on, you'll make a Fuck Budget, which will help you value and prioritize and stop giving so many unnecessary fucks now and forever.

**But before we get to not giving a fuck, let's talk about when you *should* give a fuck.**

You should give a fuck if something — be it human, inanimate, or conceptual — does not annoy and does bring you joy. Sometimes that calculation is easy and the decision is obvious. Huzzah! Very exciting. But more often — and the reason you need the NotSorry Method — you're not pausing to make any calculation at all, or you're making the wrong one.

Most people give away their fucks without much thought. Feelings of guilt, obligation, or anxiety cause them to behave in a manner that, while least objectionable to other people, is often detrimental to their own levels of annoy vs. joy.

This makes no sense and is counterproductive to living your best life. (If you don't want to be living your best life, you should just stop reading now.)

Still with me?

Okay, then, riddle me this: **Instead of feeling guilty, obligated, and anxious, wouldn't you rather feel empowered, benevolent, and carefree?** You'd be like Santa Claus, except instead of toys, you're walking around with a big ol' bag of fucks and only doling them out to the boys and girls you deem worthy.

**You can be the Santa of fucks!**

So stop saying yes right away to please others and, instead, take a moment to question not only **whether you give a fuck (i.e., care)** *about* the matter at hand but **whether it deserves a fuck (i.e., your time, energy, and/or money)** *given to* it as a line item on your Fuck Budget.

It's only after honestly answering these questions that we can allocate our fucks to the people and things, tasks and events, ideas and pursuits that annoy us least and, in turn, offer up the greatest capacity for joy.

When you think about it, life is a series of yes-or-no choices, fucks given and fucks withheld. If you continue on your current path, then at the end of each day, or week, or month, you're bound to find yourself scraping the bottom of your own personal fuck barrel — which is when you'll realize that all those fucks you gave away were for the benefit of everyone but YOU.

The NotSorry Method changes all that.

It's time to flip the script, reverse the curse, and stop giving all of your fucks to all the wrong things for all the wrong reasons.

# Not giving a fuck: The basics

**Not giving a fuck means taking care of yourself first** — like affixing your own oxygen mask before helping others.

**Not giving a fuck means allowing yourself to say no.** I don't want to. I don't have time. I can't afford it.

**Not giving a fuck — crucially — means releasing yourself from the worry, anxiety, fear, and guilt associated with saying no,** allowing you to stop spending time you don't have with people you don't like doing things you don't want to do.

**Not giving a fuck means reducing mental clutter** and eliminating annoying people and things from your life, freeing up space to truly enjoy all of the things you *do* give a fuck about.

This might sound selfish, and it is. But it also creates a better world for everyone around you.

You'll stop worrying about all the things you *have* to do and start focusing on the things you *want* to do. You'll be happier and more genial at work; your colleagues and clients will benefit. You'll be better rested and more fun around friends. You might spend more time with your family — or you might spend less, making those moments you do share all the more precious.

And you'll have more time, energy, and/or money to devote to living your best life. The people who embrace the life-changing magic of not giving a fuck are WINNING.

You want to be one of these people, don't you?

# Who are these mythical people who don't give a fuck?

In my experience, people who don't give a fuck fall into one of three categories:

Children

Assholes

The Enlightened

# Children

Children pretty much have it made. They don't give a fuck because they don't *have* to. Generally, their basic needs are being met by the adults in their lives, and even if they're not, children can barely tell the difference. Think about it: If someone else was doing your laundry all day, every day, would you give a fuck about spilling sweet potatoes in your lap or upending a yogurt cup on your head? No, you would not. If all you had to do was scream your face off to get a glass of water or a new toy, would you give a fuck about having forgotten where you put your previous glass of water or having drowned your Tickle Me Elmo in the tickle-me-toilet? Nope! And if you didn't have fully developed fine-motor skills, would you give a fuck about tying your shoes? Not in a million years.

Part of the reason children don't give a fuck is that they have no life experience. Their minds are tidy because the world's bullshit has yet to be heaped upon them. They don't *have* anything to declutter, mentally speaking.

Lucky little bastards.

But life is not fair, and they, and you, cannot remain children forever. At a certain point, we all have to suck it up and stop wearing Velcro sneakers. What you *can* do is find your way back to that magical equilibrium where the burden of adulthood is lifted by embracing the childlike zest of not giving a fuck.

## Assholes

Next up, we have assholes. Assholes don't give a fuck because they are genetically predisposed to get what they want no matter who they have to offend, step on, or — yes — fuck over along the way. (Note: some children are also assholes, but for our purposes that does not matter.) Unlike my pal Jeff, these people are not generally respected or liked. Feared, maybe, but not liked.

If being liked is important to you, then you don't want to turn into an asshole. Sure, you might free up a few nights on your calendar every week, but it won't be because you took charge of your fucks and doled them out to events you really wanted to attend and people you really wanted to see. It will be because the invitations stopped coming altogether.

No, my method is about showing you how to have everything you want — and nothing that you don't want — while *also* being thought of as a stand-up guy or gal. Which brings me to...

> **10 things assholes don't give a fuck about**
>
> 1. Other people's personal space
> 2. Making you wait
> 3. Talking in the train's quiet car
> 4. Littering
> 5. Tipping appropriately
> 6. Causing gross smells in confined areas
> 7. Using turn signals properly
> 8. Blocking the escalator
> 9. Cleaning up after their pets
> 10. Being perceived as assholes

## The enlightened

That's right. You can attain enlightenment without turning into an asshole. It's possible to revert to that childlike state of not giving a fuck, but with a self-awareness that kids just can't claim. Look, there's a long list of things I still give a fuck about (being on time, getting eight hours of sleep, artisanal pizza), and near the top of that list is being polite. Honest, but polite.

For example, if you're the kind of person who sends a handwritten thank-you note to your friends after you spend the weekend at their lake house, those same friends are unlikely to be offended when you decline their next invitation...to join them at their favorite Renaissance Faire.

It's just common sense. You like lake houses and hate Renaissance Faires? Send a thank-you note; don't be an asshole. It's a win-win!

# How can I become one of those people?

*The Life-Changing Magic of Not Giving a Fuck* is designed to help you achieve an enlightened state of essential fuck-giving **without making all the same mistakes I did.**

I'll walk you through each step, helping you inventory

your fucks and teaching you to identify whether a fuck needs giving and, if it does not, how to take action without turning into an asshole.

You see, my own journey to a significantly fuck-free life was not devoid of stumbling blocks. When I was just starting out, I stopped giving a fuck in a haphazard way; I attempted some really high-level NotSorry with regard to my friends and family — such as preemptively declining an invitation to a bris before it had been issued. I was so eager to not give a fuck about religious pageantry that I forgot I *do* give a fuck about my friend's feelings. At the very moment I sent the *Just FYI, I don't do brises* e-mail, his wife was in active labor with their firstborn son. Yikes. I'm still really sorry I did that.

I refined my approach.

**At the heart of the NotSorry Method is "not being an asshole."** After all, I didn't want to lose friends, I just wanted to manage my time more effectively so I could get greater enjoyment (and less annoyance) out of being *with* my friends.

And I found that a combination of honesty and politeness, exercised in tandem and to varying degrees (depending on what the situation calls for; see "unfortunately timed bris-related e-mails"), results in the smoothest transition to fewer fucks given.

But **the fundamental precursor to implementing my NotSorry Method** — before we even get to Step 1 or to

## Honesty and politeness: A dynamic duo

In order for you to achieve peak NotSorry in the process of not giving a fuck, honesty alone isn't going to cut it, and neither is politeness all by itself. You could be extremely honest but very rude, which means someone deserves an apology. Or you could be superpolite and a fucking liar. Polite fibbing is one thing, but if you get caught in a monster lie, I guarantee you're going to be sorry, which kinda defeats the entire purpose of the NotSorry Method. The key is to blend them into a perfect combination, like Siegfried and Roy, Hall and Oates, and Batman and Robin. Together they're capable of making magic, hitting all the right notes, and saving the day. And they never fail to complement each other, even if one shines a little brighter at times, or gets mauled by a tiger.

being honest and polite — is to stop giving a fuck about what other people think.

Let's go over that in detail.

# You need to stop giving a fuck about what other people think

If the NotSorry Method unlocks the door to life-changing magic, not giving a fuck about what other people think is how you get on the property in the first place. Otherwise, you'll be dog-paddling in the moat surrounding the Castle of Enlightenment, expending all your energy just trying to keep your head above water and fend off hungry alligators.

Not giving a fuck about what other people think paves the way toward taking Step 1 (deciding not to give a fuck). Then, you can express your decisions in a positive and productive way when taking Step 2 (not giving a fuck).

And you can do it without offending or enraging anyone! (Unless you really want to offend or enrage; sometimes that can be fun.)

But first things first.

Please listen when I say that the shame and guilt you feel when you're trying so hard to not give a fuck? It's usually not because you are *wrong* to not give that fuck. It's because you're worried about what other people might think about your decision.

And guess what? **You have no control over what other people think.**

For God's sake, you have a hard enough time figuring out what *you* think! Believing that you have any control over what other people think — and wasting your fucks on that pursuit — is futile. It is a recipe for failure on a grand fucking scale.

**When it comes to how your fuck-giving affects other people, all you can control is your behavior with regard to their *feelings*, not their *opinions*.** These are two different components related to "what other people think," which I'll discuss in depth in a moment. But for now, let's look at my method in action re: giving a fuck about things you can and cannot control.

When I was wrestling with the idea of quitting my corporate job to go freelance, I was extremely anxious about all aspects of my decision — chief among them, abandoning my "career-track" and dropping a bomb on my bank account. But I was also consumed with worry about what other people (friends, family, boss, colleagues) would think about my decision. *Is she lazy? Capricious? Suddenly too rich to work? Doesn't she care that the rest of us will have to step in and pick up the slack when she leaves?*

Now that I'm a seasoned NotSorry practitioner, I can unpack those feelings.

1. I was happy to do work — I just didn't want to do it at *that* particular job anymore. If people think I'm lazy, that's their fucking problem.

2. I gave my decision quite a lot of thought and planning, and it's nobody's concern other than mine if I didn't.

3. And no, I did not win the lottery. (But fuck you if I had — you'd quit your job too and you know it.)

In hindsight, these were relatively minor worries. The big one was whether, in leaving my job, I would knock *other people's lives* temporarily out of whack and whether they would then be upset and blame me for it.

And you know what? When you look at it that way, **I'll take "Things That Are Not My Problem" for $1,000, Alex!**

I had to decide to not give a fuck about the things I couldn't control (like how long it would take my employer to replace me) and only give fucks about the things I COULD control (like not getting up at 7:00 a.m. to leave my blissfully sleeping husband and serene park views to commute forty-five minutes via an underground B.O. factory to a job I no longer wanted to do).

Instead, I've started giving a fuck or two to things like "where my next freelance job is coming from" and "keeping my website up-to-date." But those fucks are gladly given because the freelance life brings me more sleep. And more time with my husband. And my commute is now about thirty feet, from my bed to my couch.

Once I got a handle on the difference between giving a fuck about something, and giving a fuck about what other people *think* about what I give a fuck about, it all started falling into place.

# Feelings vs. opinions

It's possible that you're hyperventilating right now. There's no shame in that. You may be thinking, *I can't possibly stop worrying about what other people think. It's programmed into my DNA!*

Well, listen: Your DNA can only take you so far. In order to live your best life, you're going to have to hack the system.

**There are two reasons you tend to give a fuck about what other people think: one, because you don't want to *be* a bad person, and two, because you don't want to *look like* a bad person.**

You should, of course, continue to give a fuck about what other people think as it pertains to their *feelings* (i.e., Are you going to actively hurt those feelings by not giving a fuck about the situation at hand?). But be honest — you know full well when you're hurting someone's feelings. Don't be an asshole.

What I'm saying is, you don't have to give a fuck about what other people think when it comes to their *opinions*. And if you can learn to speak in the **Language of Opinion**, you will find it very effective. It's honest, polite, and extremely disarming! You will neither *be* an asshole nor *look like* an asshole. And then you can stop worrying about what other people think.

Got it?

Not yet?

Okay, look at it this way: **As humans, we have every right to politely disagree with or not share someone else's opinion.** This is a passive stance. It's not hurting anybody and it's entirely defensible. You like all-natural peanut butter? Great! I don't. I think it's slimy and gross. No harm, no foul.

But say you are a friend of mine who sells all-natural, homemade peanut butter and you keep inviting me to "peanut butter parties" with sad little jars of brown goop stacked all over the kitchen counter and I'm feeling pressured to buy it for no other reason than to shut you up.

This is a watershed moment. If I don't give a fuck about all-natural peanut butter, why in God's name would I spend my hard-earned money to acquire it?

I'll tell you why: It's because I just envisioned myself saying, *Get away from me with that hippie shit, you weirdo,* which would totally hurt your feelings. And I don't want to hurt your feelings, so I'm about to give you twenty dollars in exchange for eight ounces of gunk that looks like it was masticated by a diseased elephant and then spit back out into a mason jar?

Nope, nope, nope.

**Instead, I need to tell you — honestly and politely — that I don't share your opinion that all-natural peanut butter is something I want to put in my mouth.** Thus implying that I won't be purchasing any tonight. Or ever.

Do you see what I'm getting at? I give a fuck about your *feelings,* because you are my friend (annoying peanut butter–hawking notwithstanding), but I don't have to give a fuck what your *opinion* is about my [dis]taste for all-natural peanut butter. It's no skin off my teeth if you walk away convinced that my arteries are unnecessarily clogged by trans–fatty acids because I prefer a little hydrogenated vegetable oil in my sandwich. They are my arteries, after all. So in not giving my fuck to your peanut butter, I make it about a difference of opinion.

**You can sidestep the prospect of hurt feelings entirely when you view your conflict through the lens of simple, emotionless opinion.**

NotSorry is all about simple, emotionless opinions.

However, there are many ways to skin a cat! (Eww.) And if your difference of opinion with a friend reflects a difference in core *values,* you might want to handle it with a little less honesty and an extra dose of polite. Saying you don't believe in the health benefits of organic nut spread is a little different than saying you don't believe in a woman's right to choose, or a free Palestine, or that the New England Patriots are dirty rotten cheaters.

In scenarios like these, when you don't give a fuck about the matter at hand but you also don't want to get into a fistfight or be put on a TSA no-fly list, all you really need to do is invoke the *concept* of opinions and leave it at that.

Say you're a parent, and you're always surrounded by people who have *opinions* about the way you raise your children. You probably have opinions about the way they raise theirs too, but the difference is, you keep your mouth shut about it. Anyway, parenting is hard work and people love their children unconditionally and it requires a lot of energy on your part to toe the line between cordial acceptance and seething indignation over this never-ending onslaught of unsolicited advice, which tends to be closely tied to your and other people's values and, therefore, feelings.

Then one day you're at the playground and the topic of your children sleeping in the Family Bed comes up. You're on one side of the debate (it doesn't matter which!) and a fellow parent, we'll call her Stacey, is on the other.

You don't want Stacey to think you're a bad parent for not agreeing with her over how long a kid should be able to wriggle his way under the covers and further retard Mom and Dad's post-baby boning schedule. And whichever side you're on, you don't want to actively *offend* Stacey in your disagreement, or your own child might be relegated to wandering the playground with a scarlet A for "Asshole's Kid" on his overalls.

Until today, you probably mustered a nod and smile. Maybe you even spent twenty fucking minutes listening to Stacey go on and on about the *gall* of some parents to *not* do everything the way *she* thinks it should be done. And this act of passive acceptance — not to mention twenty minutes' worth of fucks given — is eating you up inside like a gang of termites at a log party.

You need some life-changing magic, stat!

So the next time this type of thing comes up, just gaze calmly at Stacey, shrug your shoulders, and say, "I know, I know, everybody has an opinion!" Then change the subject to neutral territory, like whether George Clooney is getting hotter with age. (He is not. Peak GC hotness = *Facts of Life*–era GC.)

You've implied that Stacey's opinion is not the only one that exists, but you have given no fucks accepting or actively debating it. You didn't assault her values/hurt her feelings in the process, so you're neither being an asshole nor looking like one. You were honest and polite, and you can walk away secure in the knowledge that you don't give a fuck about what Stacey thinks and she can't fault you for anything you said.

What does that make you? NOT SORRY.

---

### On being sorry

In our society, *Sorry!* is used as shorthand for anything from "I'm not really sorry, I'm just saying that to smooth over whatever I just did/am about to do to you" all the way to a nail-biting "Oh shit, what have I done???"

And not to put too fine a gender-biased point on it, but women, especially, tend to say it way too much in an attempt to preemptively or actively defend themselves against perceived slights in the workplace, among friends, or in relationships.

When you've actually behaved badly, you should be sorry, and you should say so. And if you're about to behave badly and think that a quick *Sorry* is going to ameliorate it, you're wrong. Maybe stop being such an asshole for a change.

But if you've done nothing to be sorry about, you can (a) stop feeling sorry and (b) stop telling people you are!

In other words, the NotSorry Method achieves eponymous results. Following it encourages and enables you to act in a way that doesn't require your saying—or being—sorry at all.

---

To review: **If your fuck-giving actively affects someone else** (such as declining to purchase a friend's homemade peanut butter, or passing judgment on someone's parenting choices), be honest and polite about your decision, try to make it about a difference of opinion, and 99 percent of the time, all will be well.

**But if your fuck-giving affects you and only you** (such as not getting all tarted up just to go to the grocery store), then why should you care about what other people think? Let them have their opinions about your yoga pants and Ani DiFranco T-shirt; you're comfortable *and* you won't get hit on by the squirrelly checkout guy.

And if it's somewhere in between? Well, then you really need this book!

**It may take a little getting used to, but you must stop giving a fuck about what other people think.**

---

### Just don't be an asshole

I can't overemphasize that when done correctly, not giving a fuck does *not* mean being an asshole. As long as you contemplate your own reasons for not giving a fuck about something, visualize the effect that your lack of fucks will have on anyone else involved, and mitigate the potential for hurt feelings, you can find a solution — usually through a combination of honesty and politeness — that will stand you in good stead. And minimize the number of anonymous death threats you receive.

---

# Making a Fuck Budget

You know how satisfying it is when you spend a few months saving up for something you really want to buy, and then you go to the store and you have the money in hand and you walk out with a new snowboard or whatever?

In that moment, you're probably not giving a second thought to the things that you sacrificed over the past hundred days in order to accumulate the dollars necessary to pay for that snowboard. But you did sacrifice. Maybe you went without your Dunkin' Donuts Angus Steak and Egg Sandwich every day for three months. Or maybe you took on more hours *at* Dunkin' Donuts to make extra cash (thereby sacrificing free time). Either way, you had a goal — to save the cost of the snowboard — and you stuck to a budget relative to how much money you had to save and/or how many hours you had to work to achieve your goal.

**I suggest you implement a budget for your fucks.**

What if, instead of an in-the-moment existential crisis over whether you should just buy the goddamn peanut butter to avoid hurting your friend's feelings, you simply thought of it as a line item on your Fuck Budget?

One twenty-dollar jar of all-natural peanut butter purchased = one fuck given.

And giving your fuck to all-natural peanut butter means you have one *less* fuck to give to something equivalent — such as a twenty-dollar cab ride home from the Peanut Butter Nazi's party (so you don't have to endure the additional aggravation of public transportation). Or twenty dollars toward your snowboard. Or your rent.

That fuck is starting to seem more precious, isn't it?

**Of course, not everything is about money.** There are a lot of fucks that impose on your time or energy, if not your wallet. But you can budget your time and energy just as easily as you can budget your Benjamins.

For example, say you have a child whose peers' parents routinely bake homemade cookies for class fund-raisers. Cookies with little icing smiley faces and a separate batch of gluten-free ones for the pussies. Well, maybe you have neither the TIME nor the ENERGY to bake homemade cookies. And maybe you *do* have twenty dollars but you're worried about what the other parents will think if you contribute store-bought Oreos to the bake sale.

You see where I'm going with this, right?

You need to (a) stop worrying about what other people think and (b) budget your fucks accordingly. No time and no energy? Oreos it is!

**Too often, we allocate our fucks without a goal in sight.** We're in the moment, saying yes, making plans, agreeing to spend a weekend in Vancouver before realizing, *Uh-oh, I didn't think this through.* In order to maximize your potential for happiness, you need to consider outcomes *before* committing to giving your fucks. Your time, energy, and/or money spent should result in greater joy for you. If it is going to result in annoy, you don't want to be halfway to Canada before you figure that out. Stop. Calculate. And maybe don't give that fuck.

# What about people who can't stop giving a fuck about *you* not giving a fuck?

We all know these people. You can be as honest and polite as the day is long and they just don't get it. They can't stop themselves from arguing with you, coaxing you, and trying to change your mind. Whatever it is that you don't give a fuck about, it is so important to them that they can't accept your difference of opinion.

It could be anything from SEC football to improvisational jazz to the fact that you don't participate in your family's religious rituals. They won't be swayed by honesty or politeness. These people are begging for confrontation. **IT'S LIKE THEY WANT THEIR FEELINGS HURT.**

In cases like these, you have to consider the long-term drain on your Fuck Budget. It may actually be beneficial to be/look like a bad person if it means you can put an end to this conversation once and for all. Hey, if somebody has to tell them to fuck off, it might as well be you.

# In summation

The life-changing magic of not giving a fuck is all about prioritizing. Joy over annoy. Choice over obligation. Opinions vs. feelings. Sticking to a budget. Eyes on the prize.

Let's review the basics — the tools and processes for Deciding Whether or Not to Give a Fuck so you can proceed to Give or Not Give a Fuck:

- Does the fuck you're about to give (or not give) affect only you? Or others?

- If the former, you are *way* ahead of the game!

- If the latter, you must *first* stop giving a fuck about what other people think, before you can move on to not giving a fuck about the matter at hand.

- In order to do that, consider their *opinions* separately from their *feelings*.

- Don't be an asshole.

- Now consult your Fuck Budget: What is that fuck worth to you? Can you afford it?

- If the answer is yes, then by all means, go for it! But if the answer is no, proceed in an honest and polite fashion toward not giving a fuck and being 100 percent, bona fide NotSorry.

In case you're one of those visual learners, here is a flowchart for determining whether you should give a fuck. Feel free to refer back to it as you read on.

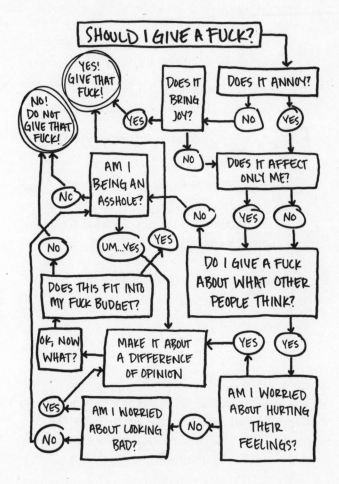

In parts II and III, I will:

- Walk you through the mental clutter you'll soon be discarding

- Teach you to pre-sort your fucks for confident, efficient decision-making

- Offer my own sample starter list of Ten Things About Which I, Personally, Do Not Give a Fuck

- Show you various strategies to implement Step 2 (not giving a fuck)

- And help you identify the things you *do* give a fuck about, all of which will allow you to achieve minimal stress, maximum happiness, and a whole lotta life-changing magic.

But for now, one last drill to get you in the zone...

# A visualization exercise

Sit down. Relax.

I want you to take a minute and do a free-form visualization of **all the things that you currently feel pressured — by friends, family, society, or even your own twisted sense of obligation — to give a fuck about.**

These could include, but are not limited to: matching your belt to your handbag, LinkedIn, eating local, hot yoga, paleo diets, the Harry Potter books, Kombucha, "trending," voting in the primaries, podcasts, ponchos-as-fashion, the Ballet, Bret Easton Ellis, hashtags, fair-trade coffee, the Cloud, other people's children, sanctimonious Christians, understanding China's economy, #catsofinstagram, *The Voice,* your father's new wife, and/or Burning Man.

Felling a tad ill, are you? Jittery, nauseous, anxious? Pissed off?

Good, then it's working.

Now visualize how happy and carefree you would be if you stopped giving all those fucks.

Hot yoga? Don't give a downward fuck!

The Cloud? Fucks not found.

And #catsofinstagram? Sorry, you're all outta fucks, meow.

Doesn't that feel so much better? I'm telling you, the moment you decide to stop giving a fuck is the moment you start living your best life.

**With that in mind, let's move on to Step 1 in the NotSorry Method: Deciding not to give a fuck.**

**11**

# Deciding not to give a fuck

In part II, we're going to take inventory of all the fucks that are cluttering up your mind. Unfortunately, it's not feasible to toss those fucks into the middle of the floor, as Marie Kondo would have you do with your socks.

But don't worry, I have ways around that.

I'll share the Four Categories of Potential Fuck-Giving, and we'll work through them one by one. It will be fun, I promise! Much more fun than your coworker's karaoke birthday party (also discussed in part II).

Ultimately, you'll make a list for each category of your mental inventory and use those lists to help you identify what annoys and what brings joy. Then, you can finish taking Step 1: deciding what you don't give a fuck about.

Once you get started, it's a very simple process. Even somewhat...addictive. I guarantee, the fewer fucks you give, the fewer you will *want* to give.

It just feels so good.

# Your mind is a barn

Deciding you don't give a fuck about something is extremely liberating. Not giving a fuck — and doing so without hurting other people's feelings or being an asshole — is even better.

But first, you have to look inward. Know thyself.

**Step 1 begins with taking inventory of your *mental* space so you can sort all the fucks being demanded of you into those that annoy and those that bring joy. Then you can decide to give or not give them accordingly.**

As I said, your fucks can't go in the middle of the floor...but *you* can.

Later, when you're ready, I'll have you sit down on the floor (hardwood is preferable — being uncomfortable motivates you to get this over with) and visualize your mind as a cluttered room. Actually, no, let's call it a gigantic barn full of crap. **That barn contains all the stuff you're being asked to give a fuck about right now, whether you *want to* or *have to,* or not.**

That barn is a big fucking mess.

(Have you seen *Hoarders*? I think I'm getting a rash.)

Next, you'll wade through your mental barn, noting all the good stuff (fucks you want to give) and all the useless clutter (the ones you don't). You might even discover some stuff you forgot you had but that deserves a place of honor in your mind/barn once you make some room. You will identify every fuck being demanded of you; you will acknowledge it and size it up and think good and hard about whether you really want and need to give it.

When you confront all of the things you're expected to give a fuck about all at once, your gut may clench, your bowels may roil, and your head and heart may begin to pound. THIS IS THE WHOLE POINT.

**We are aiming for Fuck Overload here, people.**

Most of us just poke our heads into the barn every once in a while and never get past the mountain of shit piled up just inside the door, much less do anything about the rest of it. You have to get all the way inside and really fucking *own up to it* before you have any hope of clearing it out.

Yes, you must experience Fuck Overload in order to fully recognize the time, energy, and/or money you're spending on your fucks — and to get excited about pruning them once and for all.

After you've taken a mental inventory of the barn (as I said, this happens a little later in part II), you'll make a list of all the fucks you found lurking in its depths.

**Do this once and thoroughly, and you'll have a method to free yourself for life,** even as the fucks demanded of you change over time. With the onset of holiday season, for example. You won't let that mental clutter pile up again, because you'll have the tools and perspective to keep the things you don't give a fuck about from winding up inside your mind/barn in the first place!

Again: You must list *every single fuck you find,* regardless of whether you want to give it or not. Currently, the fucks you want to and should be giving might be stacked under and behind the ones you don't — like giving a fuck about your sister's general happiness but not about the details of her new boyfriend's genital piercings.

I told you, it's messy in there. Right now, you've just got to get the lay of the land.

As Albert Einstein once said, "If I had an hour to solve a problem I'd spend 55 minutes thinking about the problem and 5 minutes thinking about solutions." Smart guy; no wonder he won a Nobel Prize.

Take the time to explore your mental barn, unearth all the fucks within, and list them one by one. I promise it will reveal the solutions for future fuck-giving and best-life-living.

Trust me on this. Or at least trust Einstein.

# Sort your fucks into categories

**In service to the NotSorry Method, I have devised Four Categories of Potential Fuck-Giving:**

Things

Work

Friends, Acquaintances, and Strangers

Family

Taken together, these categories constitute the vast miasma of people and things that you could potentially stop giving a fuck about. But we'll work through them one at a time, which will make this whole process a little easier on you. You're welcome.

**I strongly recommend that you follow my prescribed order.** Things come first in your pursuit of not giving a fuck because they are inanimate and can't talk back. Then Work, because it provokes some feeling of bitterness and resentment in nearly every person I know, which is a good motivator. Then Friends, Acquaintances, and Strangers once you've gotten your sea legs. Family comes last in your study of not giving a fuck, for what should be obvious reasons.

Look, I know you're very excited about the NotSorry Method and you're itching to tell your brother-in-law to fuck off and stop including you in his group texts about our national immigration policy — but don't give in to temptation. I can tell you that starting with Family spells doom.

I mean, Family is a fucking *minefield*.

It is, no question, the hardest thing to stop giving a fuck about. For one, there is a sense of **obligation** when it comes to family, which supersedes even **feelings** and **opinions**. This is why I recommend adding Obligations to the list of Things to potentially not give a fuck about, thereby determining your feelings about obligation before you get to a particular relative, family-related event, or memento.

Once you've tackled the early categories, it will be much easier to separate your sense of obligation toward, say, holding on to Great-Aunt Josephine's ratty fur stole from your feelings toward Great-Aunt Josephine herself (and from the feelings and opinions of your other mutual family members, who should mind their own fucking business). Hear me now, believe me later: you'll be waving good-bye to that beady-eyed beaver in the blink of an eye!

Ready?

Great, let's get this fucking show on the road.

# Things

As discussed, the Things category deals with inanimate objects and concepts, neither of which possesses the irksome *feelings* and *opinions* of your fellow human beings.

True, some items on your Things list might technically be people (I consider the Grateful Dead a *thing,* for example, though it takes the form of human bodies), and they might also technically qualify as strangers (I don't personally know any members of the Grateful Dead). But when I say *strangers,* I really mean people you've encountered but whom you don't actually know, like that guy on your vacation who's trying reeeeeally hard to get you to sign up for the time-share sales pitch and you're like, "Guy, I don't give a *fuck* about time shares *or* about whether you make your quotas." Although I guess if you already put Time Shares on your Things list, then Guy Selling Time Shares doesn't really need to go on your Strangers list — but a little redundancy never hurt anyone, especially in the pursuit of enlightenment.

Anyway...

# What are some things I may or may not give a fuck about?

If I were to make a list **today** of the things that are hanging out in my mental barn, it would include (but not be limited to):

1. Planning my upcoming vacation

2. Worrying about whether it's going to rain on my vacation

3. The fact that Donald Trump is the Republican front-runner for president

4. Finishing writing this book so I can go on my vacation

As you know, if there are items on my list that annoy, then I should not be giving my fucks to them. Vice versa with joy.

So in studying my list, I realize that I do get joy from vacation planning and writing this book, while the prospects of a Trump presidency and a rainy forecast are **not only annoying, but are also things I can't control.** Therefore, I should give my fucks to the former two and get ready to sweep the latter two out of my barn like a couple of piles of rotting hay and calcified horse manure. (But the sweeping itself is Step 2 — we'll get there in due time.)

For now, you're going to canvass your own mental barn and make a list of all the things you find in there. Maybe your list will overlap with mine, or maybe you *chose* to live in Seattle or Scotland because rain brings you joy. I don't pretend to understand that life choice, but I'm not judging you. Well, maybe a little…though by now you should know better than to give a fuck about what I think, right?

**The point is, no two lists of fucks are created equal.**

Ask yourself: What are the things you happen upon in your barn tour that make you sigh involuntarily with pleasure? How about the ones that create a feeling in your stomach evocative of a fork getting stuck in the garbage disposal?

Does it bring joy or does it annoy? When the time comes, list 'em all!

For inspiration, see below for a list of things that used to clutter my mental space and cause me no end of annoy. I've since stopped giving them my precious fucks. (This is just the tip of the fuckberg, but you'll get the idea.)

# Ten things about which I, personally, do not give a fuck

1. **What Other People Think.** Remember: This one is nonnegotiable. All fucks stem from here.

2. **Having a "bikini body."** Oh good God, the day I stopped giving a fuck about how I looked in a bathing suit, it was like a litter of kittens in black leotards had tumbled down from heaven to perform "All the Single Ladies" for the sole enjoyment of my thighs and belly. Magical!

3. **Basketball.** I have never enjoyed or understood basketball. I don't watch it, and when invited, I don't go to games. I just don't give a fuck, and my life is no worse for it. You can apply this to any sport or sports team, except the Boston Red Sox, because I said so.

4. **Being a morning person.** For most of my life I was ashamed of being useless in the early hours, of not wanting to schedule anything before noon, and of frequently arriving just in the nick of time to morning meetings. Society really seems to value morning people and look down on those of us who don't (or can't) fall in line. Once I embraced the freelance life, I stopped giving a fuck about being a morning person once and for all. Snack on it, morning people.

5. **Taylor Swift.** Everybody be all, "Tay-Tay!" and I'm like, "Nope."

6. **Iceland.** I'm sure Iceland is a beautiful country, but every time someone starts telling me about plans for their once-in-a-lifetime trip to Iceland, or about how

much fun they had in Iceland, or that "the majority of Icelanders believe in elves!" my eyes start glazing over like I'm at a Knicks game.

7. **Calculus.** This may have been my earliest recorded instance of not giving a fuck. My high-school guidance counselor insisted that I had to take this class in order to have any hope of getting into a good college. I thought long and hard about it, but ultimately determined that I did not give a fuck about calculus, and could not be bothered. I did not take the class, and I *did* get into Harvard. You can't argue with those results.

8. **Feigning sincerity.** I am the embodiment of "If you don't have anything nice to say, don't say anything at all." I just don't give a fuck about faking it.

9. **Passwords.** One of my most recent success stories. I used to give *so* many fucks and feel so much anxiety about personal security, but then I read a number of articles by experts that suggest we're all one pimply Slavic teenager away from getting hacked anyway, so I thought, *Maybe I could just use the same password for everything. Would it really matter?* Then I realized that, after sixteen years together, my husband *still* doesn't know my six-letter Hotmail password — so I could probably stop giving a fuck about devising a different Alan Turing–approved

crypto phrase for my Gap, Ann Taylor, and Victoria's Secret accounts. So far, so good.

10. **Google Plus.**\* Didn't even try it. #NotSorry.

My list may contain things about which you *do* give a fuck, and that's okay. You should feel free to slap in those earbuds and listen to "Shake It Off" on repeat while you poke around your barn.

Maybe you don't give a fuck about wearing underwear. Or the Oxford comma. Or staying to the right on a sidewalk or stairwell. (In which case, you're an asshole, or European. Perhaps both?)

Whatever — the world is your oyster!

# A few more things

As I was writing this book, I really opened the floodgates on Things I Don't Give a Fuck About (apparently I have very strong feelings about all-natural peanut butter). And while this was personally invigorating, the NotSorry novice might find it more helpful to see a list of things I *do* give a

---

\* As of this writing, even Google has stopped giving a fuck about Google Plus: http://smallbiztrends.com/2015/08/google-plus -and-youtube-separation.html.

fuck about and note how I've freed up more time, energy, and/or money to devote to them.

Remember that Fuck Budget? Here's mine, in action:

| DON'T GIVE A FUCK | | DO GIVE A FUCK |
|---|---|---|
| The threat of a nuclear Iran | → | Climate change |
| Greek yogurt | → | All of the hummus |
| "Glamping" | → | Laser hair removal |
| Lobster | → | More caviar, please |
| The pope's latest opinion | → | Reese Witherspoon's Instagram |
| Napkin rings | → | Coasters |
| The Olympics | → | Finishing season 5 of *Shameless* |
| Reading the *New Yorker* | → | Literally anything else I could be doing |
| Going to the gym | → | Sleeping |
| Taking Facebook quizzes | → | Staring off into space |
| College football | → | Campus rape |
| "Tummy time" | → | Excusing myself to get some more wine |

Some of the things on my lists might seem overly simplistic or shallow, but I assure you that they **represent a very clear and quantifiable allocation of my time, energy, and/or money.**

I often feel pressure to go to the gym, for instance, and then guilt that I never do. By deciding not to give a fuck about gym-going, I'm liberating myself from those moments of feeling guilty and inadequate (and fat), and instead joyfully indulging in an extra hour of sleep each morning. I'm reallocating time and reserving energy, and, if you factor in membership fees, I'm saving money too.

It's a No-Fucks-Given trifecta!

(I also cannot overstate the value, to me, of never having another conversation about or eating yogurt ever again. I feel so much better even just *telling* you that, honestly.)

As you work your way through the Four Categories, you're going to identify things that annoy YOU and those that bring YOU joy. Some of these revelations may cause other people to question your priorities, but who the fuck cares? **You're out there, giving fewer fucks and living your best life.**

I know I am.

Just think: In the time it took you to read this far, I've already completed a whole slew of NotSorry Step 2s. I finally stopped giving a fuck about napkin rings and the *New Yorker,* had my bikini line lasered, and spent a good deal of quality time staring off into space while the taste of creamy Sabra Classic hummus lingered on my tongue. And when the 2016 Rio Games roll around, I'll be ready to stop giving a fuck about the Olympics once and for all.

It's important to have goals.

And speaking of goals — as some poor schlub trains for ten hours a day to jump a quarter inch farther into a pile of dirt than Mike Powell did in Tokyo in 1991, it's time for you to inventory the things stacked up in your mental barn and make your first list.

I've provided columns on the next page to get you started, but feel free to move on to scrap paper.

Don't be stingy. This is important!

# THINGS I MAY OR MAY NOT GIVE A FUCK ABOUT

_____     _____
_____     _____
_____     _____
_____     _____
_____     _____
_____     _____
_____     _____
_____     _____
_____     _____
_____     _____
_____     _____
_____     _____
_____     _____
_____     _____
_____     _____
_____     _____

# Work

More complicated than the category of Things — which involves simply withholding your fucks from inanimate objects/concepts/activities — Work is still not quite as fraught as dealing with friends and family, thus making it the logical second point of entry to getting this life-changing magic under way.

Additionally, if you ask a bunch of random people what they hate most in life, lots of them are going to say their jobs, bosses, coworkers, IT departments, or something in that realm. Kind of a wide target.

Luckily, there are plenty of perfectly acceptable **ways to reduce the number of fucks you give at work** — whether it's bailing on an unnecessary meeting, eschewing useless paperwork, or declining an invitation to a coworker's party — and still continue to remain employed, respected, and even well liked (if you give a fuck about that; see page 65, "The Likability Vortex"). We'll discuss many of them in depth in this section and even more in part III.

**The two most common reasons you give too many fucks when it comes to work are:**

1. Fearing the judgment of a boss (who controls your access to a paycheck)

2. Fearing the judgment of coworkers (with whom you spend the majority of your day).

**This is all perfectly understandable on the surface, but have you ever really stopped to consider:**

1. How hard it is to *actually* get fired if you're doing a decent job?

2. How little you really care, deep down, whether Gail from Marketing thinks fondly of you? Fuck Gail and her Save the Polar Bears half-marathon fund-raising drive, am I right? (But more on Gail later.)

**For now, remember that you should only give a fuck about things you can control, and no fucks about things you can't.** Work is a petri dish teeming nine-to-five with things, people, and practices that we did not actually *choose* for ourselves and therefore cannot control.

Consider the average office building and its depressing industrial carpeting, bland conference rooms, and fake potted plants. You could let that soul-destroying tableau get you down, or…you could stop giving a fuck. Instead of walking in every day and thinking, *God, this place is a shithole in gray scale, I'm so depressed,* you could think, *At least I don't have to worry about spilling coffee on this carpet; it can't get any uglier!*

**The point is, you can only control how WELL you do your job, and how MUCH time and energy you put into it to minimize annoy and maximize joy.**

Applying the NotSorry Method to your working life and giving zero (or at least fewer) fucks to the aspects of your job that annoy can be surprisingly simple — and it does not have to result in your getting fired for incompetency or insubordination.

To get you in the right frame of mind, let's go over a few common examples of things you may or may not give a fuck about when it comes to a day's work:

# Meetings

I'm not saying you necessarily can or should completely stop attending already scheduled meetings, especially if attendance is crucial to job retention. (Assuming you want to retain your job. If not, please see "The Ultimate No-Fucks-Given to Work" on page 150.)

**But there *are* meetings you do not have to agree to attend in the first place.**

For example, say a colleague from another part of the company — the Chicago office, perhaps, if you work in San

Diego — is coming to town. Some executive assistant is "setting up meetings" wherein this colleague wanders around making the same small talk about the weather and delivering vague commentary on the state of the business in half-hour increments with everyone on your floor. There are eight meeting slots, says the executive assistant. Which one do you want?

> **PowerPoint**
>
> Steve Jobs had strong opinions about meetings too, including the use of PowerPoint in said meetings. In Walter Isaacson's biography *Steve Jobs,* the late Apple CEO argued, "People who know what they're talking about don't need PowerPoint." He's right. Fuck PowerPoint.

Answer: *None of them.*

You can just say "None of those times work for me" and continue on with your day. I know, you're worried you'll get in trouble, and your desire to stay on your boss's good side overrides your desire not to take this meeting. But if you're a competent employee and *you* know it's a pointless use of a half hour, your boss knows that too. Decide you don't give a fuck. Let someone else take one for the team. There are plenty of unenlightened coworkers who will march toward those slots like blindfolded prisoners to a firing squad. It doesn't have to be you!

(Better yet, if you have one of those e-calendars that's viewable to everyone in the office, just start marking entire days "busy" so nobody *can* schedule a meeting with you.)

Sure, some meetings are required. No way around them. But if you find those meetings to be black holes of useless chatter, not to mention a total fucking waste of your time, you could decide to not give a fuck about *paying attention*. And you can most certainly stop giving a fuck about *taking notes*. Seriously, have you ever used the notes you took in a meeting? Let's be real.

And once you've decided to stop giving a fuck about walking away from the weekly Sales Department circle jerk with a page full of meaningless doodles, you can use that time to do something you *do* give a fuck about. Such as making a grocery list. Or planning your next birding adventure (those lesser prairie chickens won't spot themselves). Or writing the Great American Novel! Just think about how much you could accomplish — stuff that you actually give a fuck about — in those currently wasted, say, one to five hours a week. **That's fifty-two to two hundred and sixty hours a YEAR.**

Yeah, I thought you'd get fired up about that.

## Conference calls

Conference calls are basically a subset of meetings. They are meetings held over the phone. They are *worse* than meetings. They are the perfect storm of nonproductivity: an excuse to get absolutely nothing accomplished and waste literally everyone's time. Whenever possible, I refuse to engage in conference calls, and I assure you I have remained a respected, productive, and employable human being.

I'm not exaggerating for effect here — I simply will not

participate in a conference call that I deem nonessential. Once I started saying no to conference calls, it was effectively like saying yes to three or four unencumbered hours per week in which I could get actual work done. **You can decide not to give a fuck about a conference call.** NOTHING OF SUBSTANCE WILL OCCUR ON IT ANYWAY. This is the nature, and paradox, of conference calls. If people persist in trying to schedule around you, make it really difficult for them and they'll give up soon enough. Seriously, if there's anything I hate more than being on a conference call, it's trying to schedule one.

And if you're worried about being a bad colleague or employee, ask yourself, *Does my not giving a fuck about being on this conference call affect other people?* The answer is obviously yes, but it actually affects them in a *positive* way. You're saving people from themselves if you gently guide them — not just yourself — away from engaging in this time-, energy-, and soul-sucking activity. Their metaphorical wallets will positively swell with extra fuck bucks!

---

### The Likability Vortex

Being liked and being respected are not necessarily the same thing. For one, it's a lot easier to keep your job if you are respected rather than merely liked. I've "liked" plenty of incompetent wastoids in my time, but I wouldn't hire them.

The Likability Vortex occurs when you care more about being liked than about being *worthy of respect*. You wind up floundering inside a devastating fucknado of your own design.

---

Why? *Because you can't control whether or not people like you.* You might be a funny person but your particular sense of humor might not jive with theirs, and they won't like you. You might be superfriendly, but they might perceive you as weird and not like you. You might be completely inoffensive, but you remind them of their ex-boyfriend AND THEY JUST DON'T LIKE YOU.

What you *can* control — by giving your fucks to the aspects of your job that make you damn good at it — is whether you are worthy of others' respect. They may or may not give it to you (they've got their own fucks to budget, after all), but if you're doing a good job, at least you know you're worthy.

And if doing a good job means spending more fucks on getting shit done and fewer on whether people like you *while* you're getting it done, then you've escaped the Likability Vortex and the fucknado that comes with it. Nice work. Take the rest of the day off.

# Dress codes

This may or may not belong on your list depending on the kind of company you work for. Obviously if you are a freelance writer, like me, you stopped giving a fuck about pants a long time ago. If you work for some fancy hedge fund or law firm or what have you, you probably have to wear a suit, no getting around it. That goes on the fucks-given list — although there's always an insouciant pocket square to increase joy. If you work retail or food service and there's a uniform, just skip this section. And if you work at an art gallery: Score! You get to do whatever the fuck you want.

But if you are one of the millions of people who work for a company that grants you permission to dress yourself each morning yet still feels the need to impose a "dress code" in the employee manual, get ready for some real talk.

My former company was very exacting about what constituted appropriate "Summer Friday" apparel: no flip-flops or thong sandals, no shorts on men or short-shorts on women, no tank tops or other "beachwear," and a few other no-no's I'm too deep into my enlightened state to remember. There were memos every year; you could set your calendar by the CEO's seasonal condemnation of bare toes. Maybe she was trying to keep it professional; maybe she suffered from podophobia. Either way, I eventually decided I didn't give a fuck.

It happened like this: Every day when I was getting dressed to commute forty-five minutes to work during the oppressive fug of summer, only to spend eight-plus hours in my office and then usually hit up a work-related event in the evening before commuting the forty-five minutes back home, I really started to resent not being able to wear *whatever the fuck I wanted.* (And also, not to brag, but I have nice feet.) If I'm going to be on those feet twelve hours a day in the sweatiest months of the year, we're talking blisters the size of poached eggs if I have to jam my stocking-free size 8s into a pair of ballet flats.

So one day in the summer of 2014, as I looked longingly at my closetful of fancy thong sandals in pretty colors that would go nicely with my work-appropriate capri pants, I just said a mental *Fuck it* and started wearing them to work.

I had spent a cumulative eight years at that company being pissed off and covered in Band-Aids from Memorial Day to Labor Day, and for what? Because I gave a fuck about the dress code! I'm getting riled up just thinking about it.

Here is what happened: NOTHING.

I wore my sandals all summer and nobody said a goddamn *word*. I even ran into the CEO in the elevator multiple times and she didn't bat an eye.

I've said it before and I'll say it again: It is very hard to get fired from a job that you're doing well. And given all the things you simply have to give a fuck about in order to actually *do* your job — there must be at least five that you could stop giving a fuck about and thereby significantly improve your day-to-day life. Dress codes are one of them.

## Useless paperwork

This one applies to so many people across the working spectrum: lawyers, bankers, secretaries, retail managers — everyone up and down the chain of command. Useless paperwork is a scourge on our society and it's up to YOU to stop giving a fuck!

Ever heard of the Broken Windows theory? Essentially, it suggests that if small infractions (like littering and vandalism) are allowed to stand, soon enough the entire environment will fall victim to larger-scale destruction.

And so it is with paperwork.

We have got to nip this shit in the bud. The more useless paperwork you acquiesce to doing, the more you'll have heaped upon you. It's, like, Newton's Fourth Law or something.

Yes, there is some paperwork you just have to fill out. Nobody gets paid if the W-9s aren't submitted. That's useful! But I'm talking about reports that you know full well nobody ever reads. That get written up and then filed away, waiting for the Apocalypse to render them even more useless. Like, TPS reports from *Office Space*–level useless. I'm talking about forms that are meant to be "circulated" but that somehow never reach their intended final resting places and have to be resubmitted seven times. And even though these forms go missing on a regular basis, the company hasn't gone out of business yet — so it stands to reason that paperwork like this is not exactly essential to operations, and you don't have to keep being a slave to it!

We all have a few such forms in our lives. I suggest you stop filling them out and see what happens. Probably nothing.

# Polar bears and half-marathons

Do you work in an office or other environment where your coworkers think it's appropriate to solicit donations for their personal activities? I did, and the only good excuse for that is Girl Scout cookies. Anything beyond Tagalongs and Samoas is a fuck you do *not* need to give.

Imagine that Gail from Marketing (remember Gail?) is soliciting pledges for her half-marathon, the proceeds of which will go to a charity that is important to Gail, but not to you. Gail is saving the polar bears or something. You couldn't give a flying fuck about polar bears. But you worry that *not* contributing to Gail's little jog-a-thon will render you a spoilsport in the eyes of your colleagues and that every time you see Gail in the break room she'll make an excuse to turn around and walk out rather than share oxygen with such a goddamn bear-hating cheapskate.

Now, ask yourself, *Do I honestly give a fuck about what Gail (or anyone else) thinks about my willingness to support her charity? About her (or anyone's) opinion of me?*

If the answer is no — which it should be, if you're taking this at all seriously — then proceed to ask yourself, *Just for the record, do I give a fuck about polar bears? How about half-marathons?*

If the answer to these follow-up questions is also no, then you've just added to your starter list of Work-Related Stuff I Do Not Give a Fuck About. Congratulations!

The next step — which we'll get to in part III — is to politely (i.e., without hurting her *feelings*) decline to contribute to Gail's pledge drive; thus you have **stopped** giving a fuck what Gail thinks, **decided** her fund-raiser is something you could not give a fuck about, and then **not given** that fuck.

**But again, you don't have to transform yourself from an overburdened fuck-giver into a jobless asshole/office pariah.**

When I say you can stop giving a fuck about what your coworkers think, I mean that, although I don't know them personally, you can probably get by with paying a *lot* less attention to their opinions about your life decisions.

As another example, let's say one of your coworkers, Tim, is having a birthday party at a local karaoke bar. For whatever reason, you don't want to go to Tim's party, but it's the kind of thing you feel pressured to attend — though it'll cost you, in the form of a good night's sleep, thirty dollars in watered-down margaritas, and/or your self-respect. Now, I'm not suggesting that you respond to such an invitation by laughing in Tim's face, or by sending him an animated GIF of that bear from *Ted* shitting into a party hat. I'm merely saying that you could — politely — decline the invitation and the world would not end. You'd have crossed one fuck off your list, and you'd have a free night as a result.

# Oh, she's got a *reputation*

Many folks that I talk to about not giving a fuck at work actually seem less concerned about hurting other people's feelings and **more concerned about hurting their own reputations.** Yet this is precisely why the NotSorry Method is *overly* concerned with not hurting people's feelings and not being an asshole. Both of those things contribute to your reputation as an employee, colleague, or boss.

The key here is preparation and finesse. You need to articulate your fucks to *yourself* — by touring your mental barn and making your lists and considering your Fuck Budget — before it comes to hurting anyone's feelings in real time. Then, act accordingly.

If you decide, for example, that you don't give a fuck about the annual company picnic, just...don't go. They can't fire you for that, and you can use those three hours to catch up on *Downton Abbey* or spend time with a loved one. (Oh, who are we kidding? *Downton Abbey* all the way.) It's not like you have to call in a bomb threat to get the picnic canceled. Just offer your regrets in a timely fashion. Honestly? Nobody cares if you're there anyway; you're kind of standoffish.

As President Obama might say, "Let me be clear." One of the things I always have given and always will give a fuck about when it comes to work — at an office job or as a self-employed ne'er-do-well — is my reputation. Budgeting my time and energy, honing my ability to focus and produce, and being respected along the way are all elements of maintaining a good reputation, which is tops on my list of Things I Do Give a Fuck About.

And if I have a reputation as someone who doesn't do conference calls? Well, that's something you should feel free to scrawl about me on the men's-room wall, alongside my phone number. I don't give a fuck. (But I do screen my calls.)

# This is not useless paperwork

As I've said, the ideal list-making state is to be sitting on a hard floor, mentally touring your barn and slowly growing numb from the hips down as you experience Fuck Overload. However, I will make an exception for the Work category if this is a list you could be making *during a meeting*. Fuck you, meetings!

Keep in mind, Work comes with a number of subcategories, such as Bosses, Coworkers, Office Politics, Meetings, Memos, etc. And then Coworkers can include sub-subcategories, such as Feelings, Birthdays, and Sick Pets.

Imagine there's a set of dented metal filing cabinets lining the walls of your barn. Yank out every drawer, one by one, and make a list of all the work-related fucks you find inside.

Then (and only then) you can move on to Category Three: Friends, Acquaintances, and Strangers.

# A note on degree of difficulty

As with hurricanes, the Four Categories of Potential Fuck-Giving get more treacherous with higher numerical designations. I have faith in your ability to withstand the onslaught, but if you're nervous about moving forward into Category Three, just know that we're talking about *extremely* practical stuff here.

Like, if you've ever sat on your couch fantasizing about how to get away with a last-minute no-show at your friend's poetry slam, you should be really excited about moving on to the next category. It might be a little uncomfortable at first, but so is listening to *The Iliad* rapped over the theme music from *Mister Rogers' Neighborhood* while you're desperate to relieve your bladder of the four glasses of warm pinot grigio you consumed just to make it that far.

# WORK-RELATED STUFF I MAY OR MAY NOT GIVE A FUCK ABOUT

| | |
|---|---|
| _____ | _____ |
| _____ | _____ |
| _____ | _____ |
| _____ | _____ |
| _____ | _____ |
| _____ | _____ |
| _____ | _____ |
| _____ | _____ |
| _____ | _____ |
| _____ | _____ |
| _____ | _____ |
| _____ | _____ |
| _____ | _____ |

# Friends, acquaintances, and strangers

We love our friends. That's why they *are* our friends. But all relationships are complicated, and sometimes friends get on friends' nerves. I do it all the time, such as when I get drunk and put things on my head and force my friends to take pictures. I realize this gets annoying, but hey, maybe they should leave quietly before I get to my fifth glass of wine! And this is exactly why it's important to develop your internal strategy for not giving a fuck when it comes to conflicts that could put significant strain on — or even destroy — a friendship.

The thing is, other people deposit a lot of *their* fucks in *your* mental barn. Some of these are short-term storage. Some have been gathering dust in a back corner for years. But the real question is, how did those fucks get there in the first place?

Oh, that's right. You let them in.

# Setting boundaries

In your quest not to be annoyed by friends, acquaintances, and even strangers, you need to set some boundaries around your barn.

Maybe these are invisible boundaries, like those electric shock fences people set up to keep their pets from escaping. For example, say that every time you go to a certain couple's house, their giant, slobbery dog tries to lick your balls like they're made of Alpo, and you want to avoid going there so you can avoid being *annoyed* at your friends by way of their ball-licking dog. You don't give a fuck about dealing with their dog, but you don't want to tell them this because you suspect it will hurt their feelings. You're so polite! So you set a private boundary: you invite them to come to you, or suggest neutral hangout spots where your balls can remain out of harm's way. And if they have a gathering at their house, maybe you get a little tummy ache that night. There's no harm in pleading gastric distress every once in a while to keep a friendship intact.

Sometimes your boundaries can be more obvious, like a tasteful No Trespassing sign, or that fancy coiled wire they string up around prison yards.

For example, early in my development of the NotSorry Method, I was confronted with the Pub Trivia Problem. I have a group of friends who just *loooooove* pub trivia. In

Williamsburg! (For those who don't know — Williamsburg, Brooklyn, is a godawful hipster wasteland populated exclusively by mustaches and empty cans of Pabst Blue Ribbon.) They kept asking me to join them, and I kept making lame excuses not to go. Then I would have to remember what my excuse was lest I get caught out on Facebook during pub trivia "GETTING MY NAP ON."

But once I embraced NotSorry, instead of racking my brain to come up with yet another lame excuse — and then having to self-police my social media to make sure I didn't get caught in a lie — the next time they asked, I just said, "You know what? I really don't like pub trivia, and I'm not big on Williamsburg either, so my answer to this is always going to be no. I should probably just tell you that now and save us all the Kabuki theater of invitation and regrets."

I erected my fence and it worked like a charm!

**Are you worried that your friends will be mad at you if you just tell them the polite truth?** Then you worry too much. The beauty of the NotSorry Method is that you won't *have to* worry, because you've taken everyone's feelings and opinions — including yours — into consideration before acting.

Now that my friends know the truth, I feel Liberated with a capital *L*. I was honest and polite, and nobody's feelings got hurt so I didn't have to apologize. I was quite literally not sorry.

Plus — major win — I didn't have to go to pub trivia in Williamsburg.

Those first two were pretty easy, straightforward examples, but we're just getting started. There will be plenty of things on your Friends list that are going to require more complex NotSorry, which is why I also included Acquaintances and Strangers in the Category Three mix. This way, if you get stuck on whether to give a fuck about your friend's "divorce shower" or the truly insignificant injury that she won't shut up about (ankles twist, Susan, that's what they do), you can practice your method on a chatty neighbor or a grocery-store checkout clerk, then work your way up to fucks given/not given to your nearest and dearest.

Which brings me to…

# Solicitations, donations, and loans, oh my!

We touched on this briefly with Gail from Marketing, but the request for money in the guise of a donation to a cause or someone's pet project — or even as a cash loan — happens even more regularly among friends. You know what I'm talking about: a hundred-dollar-a-head fund-raiser for someone's political-candidate-of-the-moment, a fifty-dollar pledge to someone else's bike ride for feline obesity, or twenty-five dollars toward a Kickstarter campaign for "the perfect kazoo."

You can put Kickstarter (and Indiegogo, PledgeMusic, GigFunder, RocketHub, GoFundMe, etc.) on your Category One list of Things I Don't Give a Fuck About, but that naked plea for cash and validation is always attached to a person. It could be from a close friend, a social media–level acquaintance, or, in many cases, a stranger with whom you share a mutual friend who felt guilted into forwarding it to you and three hundred other unsuspecting rubes. These things are Category One with Categories Two through Four rising. Very sneaky.

Anyway, I don't mean to delegitimize such requests, which are typically made in good faith. But while there are plenty of excellent causes, charities, and inventions out there that may be worthy of your dollars and fucks — I myself have contributed to several — **I'll hazard a guess and say they cannot ALL possibly fit within your Fuck Budget.**

And that, my friend/acquaintance/stranger, is why you're reading this book!

The Internet has made possible such glorious innovations as Tinder and online mah-jongg, but it has also brought out the panhandler in many of us by way of e-mail, social media, and crowdfunding websites. **These avenues make it much easier and less confrontational for people to ask you for money.** If all the requests I received over e-mail or Facebook had to be made in person with a clipboard and a fanny pack to hold old-fashioned cash donations, I promise you half of these folks would never be biking to cure feline obesity or trying to invent that kazoo.

In one year, for example, urgent requests for donations to cure AIDS, diabetes, and heart disease; support Planned Parenthood; fund one podcast, two independent films, and three music albums; eradicate four different cancers; and subsidize several doomed entrepreneurial endeavors made their way into my social media feeds or e-mail in-box. **Some from close friends, some from friends of friends, and some from — yes — total strangers.**

Before I started down my path to enlightenment, I spent far too many valuable minutes agonizing about whether to contribute to any/all of these charitable appeals, and then too many dollars donating to them. **But it wasn't just about the time and money.** I also spent a lot of energy worrying about who would know whether I did or didn't contribute, and what they would think of me. And also whether I would have to fucking *talk* to them about it at a party someday, tail between my stingy little legs.

No more!

Now that I'm a practitioner of the NotSorry Method, I can quickly and easily determine whether I give a fuck about the request itself and whether it affects anyone else, then act on my decision in an honest, polite way that leaves me with more time, energy, and money to spend on other things. I can padlock my barn door and unlock it only to bring in the fucks that I (a) have room for and (b) am happy to store for you for a night, a couple weeks, or in perpetuity.

Have I mentioned that my method is both simple and life-changing?

**Let's start with strangers and acquaintances and work our way up the ladder to friends, one needy rung at a time.**

Say one day you get a mass e-mail from a low-level acquaintance who obviously just cc'd his whole address book asking you to "contribute what you can!" to his old summer camp friend's fund-raiser for . . . I don't know . . . sunglasses for dogs.

Reviewing what you've already learned, you determine that while this line item on your Fuck Budget does affect someone else, it does so in a pretty indirect way — you're not actively taking anything away from this aspiring entrepreneur (who is a complete stranger to you), you're just not adding to their coffers.

Second, the person who sent you the request is just an acquaintance, not a close friend, so you probably don't have to explain yourself — or your **difference of opinion** about whether the world needs sunglasses for dogs — in person anytime soon.

Last, this isn't a situation where, if handled properly, anyone's **feelings** are going to get hurt. I mean, you shouldn't Reply-All to the whole e-mail list saying, *Sunglasses for dogs? That's the stupidest idea since Baby Bangs!\** There's no need to be an asshole about it. (Although, for the

---

\* http://baby-bangs.com/index2.php.

record, both of those are very stupid ideas. What the fuck does a six-month-old need with hair extensions?)

So, Step 1: When all is said and done, do you give a fuck about sunglasses for dogs?

No? Then why haven't you already deleted that e-mail, you sucker? (I'm sorry, but that was too easy.)

**Fine, fine, but that was just a random friend of a friend. What happens when a really close friend wants you to donate to something that's really important to her?**

This is when you have to dig deep and use all of your tools. Wax on, wax off, paint the fence, etc. (Mr. Miyagi... now there was a guy who gave no fucks.)

First question: Is your friend's project really important to you too? Does it, you know, "spark joy"? If the answer is yes, and you can fit a donation into your actual budget, not just into your Fuck Budget, then go with God. Why are we even having this conversation?

But if the answer is no, ask yourself whether it's possible to decline (honestly and politely) without hurting your friend's feelings. Depending on what kind of person your friend is, that could be easy or not-so-easy.

Will you never have to speak of it after that initial e-mail volley? Then proceed to Not Giving a Fuck. Do not pass Go, do not deposit $200 in your friend's Kickstarter.

Or is your friend likely to bring it up in casual conversation when you see her? ("OMG, my Kickstarter is seventeen percent funded! CAN YOU BELIEVE IT WINK-WINK NUDGE-NUDGE?!") In this case, you should reply with something like "That is so great! I'm so happy for you!" meanwhile thinking, *I am not acknowledging that I haven't contributed unless you ask me outright, you coward.*

In situations like these, you are like a master of the Chinese martial art tai chi, the general principle of which is to yield to an incoming attack rather than meet it with opposing force. In doing so, you absorb your opponent's energy and redirect it back at her so that she is essentially vanquished by her own hand. **In other words, you can politely respond to her passive-aggression with a dose of your own and win this battle without your friend even realizing that you've fought.**

It gets a little trickier — but not impossible! — if your friend is one of those people who can't be placated with a gentle sidestep and some ancient Chinese philosophy. This is when you have to whip out your Fuck Budget and your opinions vs. feelings calculator in the middle of the party and develop your honest, polite response about how you're *super*happy for her, and you hope she understands that you don't have extra money to spend in pursuit of anyone else's hopes and dreams.

*Et voilà.*

Go ahead, say it. You don't think it's going to work, do you?

You acknowledge that in the end you might save yourself the actual monetary donation, but you don't *really* believe you'll save yourself much agonizing over what your friend thinks or over the prospect of hurting her feelings.

You think I haven't been there? Well, I have, and that's why I've got a little something else in my trick bag for you...

# Personal policies

**Personal policies are an excellent way to conserve your fucks swiftly, efficiently, and with an extremely low risk of hurt feelings.** (Listen, I can't help you if your friend is *that* much of a self-involved basket case — maybe she should consider therapy.)

Here's how it works:

If there's something I don't give a fuck about but that exists in that gray area of potentially hurting someone else's feelings no matter how honest and polite I am, I simply chalk it up to a "personal policy."

As in "I have a personal policy against donating to Kickstarter campaigns, because if I donate to one, I feel like I have to donate to them all. I just can't afford it, and if I had to choose, I wouldn't want anyone I love to think I value them more or less than anyone else."

Zing!

And as I said, **you can include any/all charitable donations, pledges, and even cold-hard-cash loans in this category of fucks,** since they are typically solicited in the same manner, by the same people, and can be covered by the same personal policy.

Say it one more time, with feeling:

**"I have a personal policy against _____, because if I _____ one, I feel like I have to _____ them all. I just can't afford it, and if I had to choose, I wouldn't want anyone I love to think I value them more or less than anyone else."**

Now, imagine you're on the other end of that response. You might get a little huffy for a hot second, but can you really...argue? No, you cannot. At least, not without being an asshole. (See what I did there?) And you certainly shouldn't take it *personally*. It's just my policy — which is kind of like my opinion but even harder for anyone to argue with because as human beings, we are conditioned to submit to things like "rules" and "policies."

Told you this wasn't my first rodeo.

# Things you might have a personal policy against

### Second-wedding bachelor/-ette parties

Simply uncalled-for.

### Dispensing free professional advice

I'm sorry, do I look like someone who doesn't charge good money for the expertise I spent eight years in grad school and $230,000 in college loans accumulating?

**Breakfast meetings**

Useful for avoiding dates with sober people and small children.

**Driving more than four hours round trip in the same day**

"Back problems."

**Karaoke**

It's kind of appalling how many times and in how many ways a personal policy against karaoke will save your ass.

**Potluck dinners**

Seriously, what the fuck is wrong with people.

**Documentary films**

This is the most common kind of film your friends will make, trust me.

**Poetry slams**

If you never RSVP yes in the first place, you won't have to agonize over a last-minute cancellation, now will you?

# RSVP'ing no means no

Let's look at a personal policy in action:

Say a close friend invites me to be his date for a gallery opening with an artist Q&A after. I really, really don't give a fuck about gallery openings — like, the very idea of going to one makes me want to slit my wrists with a toothpick I just pried out of a stale cheese cube—but he's very sensitive and artsy and I don't want to risk hurting his feelings, so I tell him I have a personal policy against gallery openings.

And maybe I look down and sort of visibly shudder, just to really drive it home. For all he knows, I got gonorrhea at the last gallery opening I went to. Nobody wants to discuss that.

In my experience, people don't tend to push too hard once you serve them with a personal policy (especially when it's delivered with a certain flair). If I were to say, "Oh, I don't really like gallery openings," then that's just my opinion—and although it's valid and I could stand my ground with confidence, opinions are easier to debate than policies. And you might have to get into it a little, eating up valuable time and energy:

"You don't like gallery openings? Why not?"

"Well, I think they're kind of boring and my feet hurt from standing."

"But you get to commune with the work under halogen lighting!"

**Plus, there's always your friend's pesky _feelings_.**

"Yeah, but it always gets so stuffy in there. I don't think artsy people wear deodorant."

"Um, what exactly are you implying? I *smell* bad? God, you're being a real asshole, you know that? You could have just said no."

"I did. But then you argued with me. You realize we're still talking about this, right?"

Personal policies are definitely the way to go in this scenario. They are mysterious and they tend to make people a little bit uncomfortable and really shut down the conversation. Like Kanye.

And the even better thing about developing a personal policy is that it's your policy, so you can amend it or suspend it whenever you want—and nobody wants to argue with you because *they're* afraid of hurting *your* feelings!

That's some real ninja shit right there. Mr. Miyagi would be proud.

# The tiny little elephant in the room

We've done very good work so far, have we not? We've engaged in some hard-core visualization, learned the difference between feelings and opinions, practiced the art of not giving a fuck about what other people think, scrutinized our Fuck Budgets, and gotten the lowdown on personal policies (a *personal* favorite). I can practically feel the life-changing magic bubbling up within you.

Which of course means it's time to throw you a curveball.

Not giving a fuck isn't necessarily easy. Simple, yes. Easy, not always. And that's precisely why we're building a solid foundation of lists and practice scenarios and related concepts to shore up your defenses for the really tough stuff.

**Like children.**

Which friends, acquaintances, and strangers seem to have in endless supply.

(I'm not talking about your nieces and nephews and cousins and kids and grandkids — they all belong in Category Four: Family. That's a whole other ball of placenta. Right now, we're focused on identifying the things you can reasonably be expected to not give a fuck about as relates to children *who are not related* to you.)

**If you're a nonparent, it can be daunting to admit you don't give a fuck about child-related things.** People's feelings about their children are so emphatic and visceral (and occasionally irrational) that it can be hard to accurately predict whether — in your quest to not give a fuck about toddler birthday parties — you are going to hurt someone's feelings, or whether that person will accept your difference of opinion and let you off the hook.

None of this changes the fact that getting up at nine

o'clock on a Sunday morning to watch a one-year-old smear cake on his face is something you decidedly don't give a fuck about — but you might still be understandably trepidatious about proceeding to Step 2, not giving a fuck.

That's what I'm here for.

As you may have already inferred, I am, shall we say, immune to the charms of children. But through long experience — and because parents tend to feel comfortable confiding their shameful little secrets to a childfree pal over a few bottles of wine — **I can tell you that even parents don't always give a fuck about kids other than their own.**

As one mother put it, "It's about a funneling of fucks, really. All of my fucks have been funneled toward *my* child. I have none left over for you or for how you do it."

So, just to make absolutely sure that this book contains appropriate levels of life-changing magic for *everyone*, **I canvassed parents nationwide to find out exactly what THEY don't give a fuck about, and why.**

It was all extremely illuminating, and I will share it with you in due course.

But I also want to acknowledge that, as cathartic as it was (and it clearly was) for these parents to tell me about all the fucks they don't give with regard to pee and pacifiers, there were plenty who added the caveat that so much about having kids *is* rewarding and worth giving a fuck about.

And that's the key: **giving your fucks to the things that**

**make you happy** — like reading or cooking or playing with your mini-me — **and not giving a fuck about the rest.**

One mother responded from the perspective of teaching her own kids what to give a fuck about: "As someone who grew up in a household full of guilt, I think it's important for our kids to know that they can make decisions about what to care about, and that they don't need to pay attention to the approval or condescension of other people in deciding how to live their lives."

Right on!

And perhaps the most practical comment came from a mom who said that having a child can actually serve you well in prioritizing fucks given to *other* areas of life, such as the workplace. That the well-being of this brand-new human can sometimes be the catalyst to finally *stop* giving a fuck about staying after hours, taking on added responsibilities, and pinch-hitting for the real or metaphorical company softball team. It can lead you to draw clear boundaries with supervisors and employees alike and to be honest and firm about what you're capable of handling in any given day.

In other words, that precious creature could be your first step in adopting the NotSorry Method, Category Two: Work. *Boom!*

Without further ado, I am pleased to present the following:

# Things even parents don't give a fuck about

**From where your baby emerged**. Natural, drug-free vaginal birth? More power to you. Cesarean? Keepin' it tight. Water birth? Whatever floats your boat. Another woman entirely? Isn't science great! Regardless of the provenance of your bundle of joy, most people don't give a fuck, so you can stop feeling the need to defend your epidural in mixed company.

**Whether you choose to breast-feed or not**. Although the comments sections of some Facebook walls might suggest otherwise, as it turns out, the majority of parents care only about their own kids' suckling habits and do not give a fuck about whether your darling newborn has successfully "latched," how chapped your nipples may or may not be, or if baby's immune system will suffer from being raised on formula. You do you, Mama.

**Ferberizing**. You don't have to justify it or decry it to anyone. Nobody cares how your kid goes the fuck to sleep. Just git 'er done!

**Sharing**. Most parents do want their children to grow into adults who understand the concept of sharing and know when it's the right thing to do. Just like they want them to grow up not to be serial killers. But perhaps everyone fixates on sharing a little too much when it comes to this or that toy or book or hat. As one mother said, "It would be lovely if my son wanted to share his truck [with your child], but I don't ask you to give me a slurp of your eight-dollar iced coffee at the playground, do I? You can shoot me various imploring/judgmental/evil looks while your kid cries over someone else's toy — I am taking ten minutes to read my phone in peace while my child is blissfully occupied with the toy I bought him."

**"What the experts say."** Parents know what the experts say — they all read the same wildly conflicting books and articles and studies when deciding whether to let Junior handle an iPad for ten minutes a day before his fifth birthday. And they may give a fuck about what the experts say — or not — but they certainly don't need to hear it all over again from *you,* a 100 percent certified nonexpert.

**Potty training.** Some parents like the feeling of camaraderie/schadenfreude that accompanies talk of potty training — it helps them feel less alone. Maybe they score some good tips or maybe they get to feel superior for having a kid who takes to the porcelain throne with ease. But on the whole, there are very few people on this earth who give a fuck about the details of when, where, under what circumstances, and how often a child excretes waste from his or her lower half. Gross.

**Naps, scheduling of.** It would appear from my research into this topic that many parents remember that *they* fell asleep anywhere and everywhere as kids, and yet modern child-rearing texts would have them believe that naps must happen on a schedule as strict as a Béla Károlyi training regimen if they are to have any hope of ANYONE SLEEPING EVER AGAIN. Which is a perfectly understandable concern—there's a reason sleep deprivation is a form of torture. But, you know, maybe we don't have to *talk* about it quite so much? One mom told me that every time her friends start detailing little John's and Janie's nap schedules, she'd much rather be talking about books, or politics, or her latest sex dream, or Matthew McConaughey's arms (which may have featured prominently in said dream). *Alright, alright, alright.*

**"Whether anyone thinks I should keep trying until I have a [child of a different sex than the three I already have]."** I heard this from several moms and, I mean, it's essentially a fifty-fifty proposition every time, right? So...are the people who ask this ridiculous question going to keep taking the wrong-gender babies off mommy's hands until she hits the jackpot?

**Parental one-upmanship.** Nobody but you gives a fuck about what AMAZING programs your child's school offers (Robotics! Mandarin! Trapeze!), or how many hours of homework the teachers assign, or the intricacies of your chauffeur schedule. Nonparents especially don't give a fuck, but other parents only want to know this stuff if they are considering sending their own kids to that school, or carpooling with you.

Parents! Who knew? I feel so much better about all the fucks I never gave to any of this stuff, and I hope you do too.

Finally, to round out Category Three, I have a piece of tried-and-true advice that may run contrary to everything you've read thus far — but as we know from the fact that Nick Nolte was once named *People's* Sexiest Man Alive, there is no rhyme or reason to this world...

# Sometimes it's okay to hurt people's feelings

Oh, don't look so shocked. It's true that until now I've staunchly advocated using "other people's feelings" as a barometer for deciding whether you give a fuck and, more important, to consider them when acting on Step 2 of the NotSorry Method, not giving a fuck. Honesty, politeness, not being an asshole. You know the drill.

But when it comes to Category Three strangers (and even the occasional acquaintances), I gotta tell you: sometimes you just can't worry about whose feelings are getting hurt in pursuit of living your best life.

**Not giving a fuck — and reserving your fucks for what's really important to you — is an evolving process.** It means prioritizing your fucks based on what comes at you every day. And there are going to be days when hurting some stranger's feelings is low on the totem pole.

*Real low.*

I'm not saying you should start tweeting insults at strangers just for you-know-whats and giggles. Or walk out into the street and exhort random passersby to "suck a bag of dicks" (™ Louis C.K.). That is not life-changing magic. That is just mean.

But some time, some day, in your heart of hearts, you will know when it is okay to hurt someone's feelings in the process of not giving a fuck. Economists call it an opportunity cost. I call it common sense.

## A few scenarios in which it is okay to hurt a stranger's feelings in the process of not giving a fuck

1. **When people knock on your door trying to convert you to their religion.** You do not — I repeat, do

*not* — have to feel bad about closing it right in their faces. True, you can't spell P-R-O-S-E-L-Y-T-I-Z-E without P-O-L-I-T-E, but that's just semantics.

2. **When the person in line ahead of you at Starbucks can't make up her mind and you are legit in a hurry.** I hereby grant you permission to inquire, "So...are you nearsighted? Because I would be happy to recite the menu in its entirety for you, a process that cannot possibly take longer than we have already been standing here waiting for you to make some pretty basic life decisions."

3. **When the lady or gentleman onstage at the comedy club is absolutely the *antithesis* of funny.** It's one thing to be polite; it's another thing to endure twenty minutes of stale jokes and staler beer. He or she chose this career path — he or she better have feelings of steel. Don't give a fuck; walk out, and don't look back.

4. **When other women pee on the seat.** These monsters deserve to be actively shamed. My Fuck Budget does not account for time spent gingerly wiping off *your* urine before I can sit on a public toilet, and I am too short to squat effectively. I will follow you back out into that bar/stadium/conference room/banquet hall and I will give you a stern talking-to, yes, I will.

5. **When someone leans his airplane seat back into your knees.** I don't give a fuck about your personal space if you don't give a fuck about mine, buddy. I may not hurt your feelings but I will kick you in the back for as long as it takes.

So there you have it: Plenty of tools to decide whether giving a fuck about various scenarios involving friends, acquaintances, or strangers is in your future. Time to get down on the floor, scavenge around in your mental barn, and make your list!

## FRIENDS, ACQUAINTANCES, STRANGERS, AND RELATED ITEMS I MAY OR MAY NOT GIVE A FUCK ABOUT

| | |
|---|---|
| _____ | _____ |
| _____ | _____ |
| _____ | _____ |
| _____ | _____ |
| _____ | _____ |
| _____ | _____ |
| _____ | _____ |
| _____ | _____ |
| _____ | _____ |
| _____ | _____ |
| _____ | _____ |
| _____ | _____ |
| _____ | _____ |
| _____ | _____ |
| _____ | _____ |

# So... do I have any friends left?

We've been dwelling on the negative for a while here to help you get to the heart of what you honestly just don't give a fuck about. But **the whole purpose of making these lists** and crossing out things that threaten to overdraw your Fuck Budget **is to reveal the ones that are worthy.** And to create more time and emotional space to preserve and pursue those relationships and all the fucks they entail. That's the life-changing magic in a nutshell.

Part IV is where all of this will be synthesized, but before we get there, we have a bit more work to do.

Yep, it's time to blow the barn doors off the mother of all fuck-giving.

# Family

Oh, family.

Oh, *them*.

Where to begin? Like the IRS, your family exists to fuck with you. Family—and all its group photos, weddings, bar and bat mitzvahs, christenings, quinceañeras, all-inclusive vacations, group-therapy sessions, right-wing uncles, sibling rivalries, drama, and grudges—promotes constant, daily fuck-giving.

Like the certain (some might say, inordinately large) percentage of your income that automatically goes to taxes, **a certain percentage of your fucks go straight to Family.** And on top of that, somehow the consequences of those fucks given (or not given) seem weightier than those derived from Things, Work, and Friends/Acquaintances/Strangers combined. It's like we're all afraid of being audited by our cousins.

*Why is that?* you ask. I have one word for you: **Guilt.**

**Once you feel guilty, you have already failed at not giving a fuck.** Game over. Because feeling guilty means you have not been able to effectively use the tools and perspective I've taught you to not only not give a fuck, *but to feel happier doing it.*

Guilt is not a happy feeling. It's more like that feeling

when you have a sudden, agonizing itch in your crotch area but you're surrounded by people and you can't dig in after it and you're just *dying* to get some relief. That is what guilt feels like.

**Not giving a fuck should always result in greater pleasure, satisfaction, and happiness. Not crotch itch.**

Which makes it even more important to study the NotSorry Method and use every tool at your disposal to unplug the family guilt machine before it can suck you in and spit you out like that Nordic assassin did with a corpse and a wood chipper in *Fargo*.

If at all possible, try to steer clear of that outcome.

As you may recall, earlier in the book I talked a little bit about obligation and how it pertains to family. It is a truth universally acknowledged that family members tend to think other family members **have to give a fuck about their lives just because they share DNA.**

Think about that for a second. Does it make any sense at all? No, it does not.

**One of the central tenets of fuck-giving is choice over obligation.** You want to be able to *choose* how to spend your time, energy, and money so that you maximize the enjoyment of any given relationship, task, product, or event. **Things you can control vs. things you can't.**

And as we all know, you don't get to choose your family. So at the very least, you should get to choose *how and why you interact with them*. Right?

Right?!?

Sigh.

Well, let's at least give it a shot.

# When a cigar is not just a cigar and a teacup is not just a teacup

Let's say your mother, bless her nostalgic, micromanage-y little heart, is trying to unload her mother's (your grandmother's) Royal Heidelberg china on you, and you really don't want it. You feel this affects only you, because you're the one who has to store it and pretend to like it and use it when your parents come over — but you know that in reality it affects your mother too, because she is affected by literally everything you do. (You came out of her *vagina*.) So if you refuse to accept this "gift" from the woman who squeezed you through her tender young cervix, you are almost certainly going to hurt her feelings.

**So... time to drop "opinions vs. feelings" on her, right?**

Ah, but even though it is really just your mother's *opinion* that you should care about the family china, she can't separate that from her *feelings* about her mother/your grandmother, who will never even know you have the teacups in your possession, because she is dead. (My condolences.)

You then run multiple scenarios in your head and determine that it's hopeless because even if you are honest and ultrapolite, your mother is likely to have her feelings hurt no matter what you say. You conclude that you should suck it up and pretend you give a fuck about the teacups.

This frustration is common when dealing with family. You just want to throw up your hands and submit because **OBLIGATION** and **GUILT.**

I'm here to tell you, there are alternatives.

Of course, I can't claim to absolve you of *all* guilty inclinations toward your family — that's what prescription benzodiazepines are for — but this section of the book will help you determine which aspects of your family life are truly fuck-worthy and/or nonnegotiable. Yes, sometimes you just have to suck it up and give a fuck when it comes to family, but I can show you how to reframe your fucks to get the most out of a less-than-ideal situation. Remember: you are a part of your family, and you deserve to be happy too.


# Survey says...

As it turns out, we all share many of the same opinions when it comes to things we don't give a fuck about with regard to our families. I know this because I conducted an anonymous survey asking people to name something about their families that features high on their No-Fucks-Given list, and even I was shocked at how many overlapping responses cascaded in. (I told you family was a fucking minefield.)

So let's play our own version of everyone's favorite game show where moms make uncomfortable, vaguely lewd on-air banter with Steve Harvey...*FAMILY FEUD!*

The question in my survey was "Name something about your family that you don't give a fuck about." Read on for the top six results, from least to most popular.

## 6) The fact that we share a bloodline as though that pertains to something you are trying to convince me to do

About five minutes ago, I declared that it makes no sense whatsoever to give a fuck about anyone or anything *just because of your genetic link to that person or thing*. With the exception of your own offspring, who you kind of owe since you brought them into this world — at least until they're old enough to fend for themselves — you are simply not obligated to give these fucks. You might *think* you are. But you are not. And a lot of you seem to know that already, so maybe there's hope for you after all.

## 5) Mandated togetherness/"liking" of all family members

Each of us is a pretty, pretty snowflake. No two exactly the same. Even identical twins! (It's true; look it up.) So how in the name of Gemini can we all be expected to like one another all the time and want to hang out constantly? Family members who enforce unwanted togetherness among siblings or cousins or grandchildren who don't like one another are giving a fuck about all the wrong things.

## 4) Group photos

I wasn't expecting this to rank so high, but, boy oh boy, do people hate taking group photos with family. The point, it seems to me, is that very few of you give a fuck about the photo itself. You'll see it on Facebook tomorrow, click an obligatory "Like" and then forget about it. We no longer live in a world where people spend quality time on Friday night swilling gin martinis and poring over family photo albums. (Did anyone ever live in that world?) The inherent disregard for the photo is compounded by — as many responders indicated — the fact of the photo being taken "last minute" (nobody likes a sneak attack) or by "being forced to dress alike" (nobody wants to look like a member of an Australian shampoo dynasty*). Again, this is a numbers game; if a good chunk of family members don't

---

* I can't be the only one who remembers these disturbing ads for Aussie hair care, can I? http://i1.wp.com/www.themysticwave.com /wp-content/uploads/2015/05/Aussie_Brand.jpg.

want to pose for the formal group photo, they ALL need to man up and decide not to give a fuck. Majority rules!

## 3) Ancient history

*Sibling rivalries, grudges, petty arguments,* and DRAMA!!! populated the survey like "famous" potato salad recipes at a family reunion. It's pretty clear that nobody gives a fuck about who said what, whose fault it was, or which one of us Mom likes better. (Hi, Tom! Thanks for reading my book.)

## 2) Outdated holiday or other family traditions

As families grow and relatives die off, so should some traditions. And yet, many of us seem to be locked into a *Groundhog Day*–style malaise when it comes to annual events and outdated rituals related to holidays, vacations, and other family gatherings. Thanksgiving might as well be renamed "Fucksgiving." Religious holidays like Christmas, Easter, and Hanukkah are double the dogma, double the fucks. That rustic cabin your dad has rented every Labor Day since 1986? Thirty years later, it's now so dilapidated that you'd be better off skipping the vacation and spending the weekend with your own kids in the ER getting tetanus shots. In the same way that "just because we're related doesn't mean I have to give a fuck about X," just because this is how your family has always done something doesn't mean this is how you have to do it until the end of time. A respectful difference of opinion delivered with a little honesty and politeness could do wonders for you here. Or, if all else fails, a personal policy against rustic cabins.

Finally … drumroll, please … the number-one response to "Name something about your family that you don't give a fuck about."

Well, it was a tie.

## 1) Religious and political differences

That these two ideological quagmires were put forth over and over and over again by the survey participants means they each merit a good old-fashioned NotSorry breakdown.

Let's start with religion. It'll be like an exorcism. A fucksorcism, if you will.

# Am I my brother's keeper?

This is a classic case of getting back to our roots, and to that very first element of the NotSorry Method: deciding not to give a fuck about what other people think. Your religious views affect you and only you—same goes for your aunt Jennifer in all her Southern Baptist glory, glory, hallelujahs. She has her opinions, you have yours. If you are honest and polite about your difference of opinion and you request that religion no longer be a topic of discussion among family, you are not being an asshole. You are being reasonable, and if anyone gets his or her feelings hurt, it's not your fault.

**Let me give that the "Robin Williams in *Good Will Hunting*" treatment:**

It's not your fault.

It's not your fault.

IT'S NOT YOUR FAULT.

So the next time Aunt Jennifer makes a not-so-subtle reference to your proclivity for living in sin with your girlfriend, just wipe the eggs Benedict off your chin and say, "I respect your opinion, Auntie J, but I would prefer not to have a conversation about our religious differences here at Mimi and Paw-Paw's sixtieth-wedding-anniversary brunch."

How honest and polite was that? You are *so* not the asshole here.

Just try it. You might be surprised at how well it goes over. Or at least at how totally caught off guard she is and therefore unable to respond with more than a nervous titter and the raising of one overplucked eyebrow.

**The power of honesty cannot be overrated. I can't tell you how many *more* fucks you wind up giving when you**

**try to beat around the bush. God, even that expression sounds exhausting.**

The thing is, I'm guessing you haven't even *tried* this method before because you got so caught up in the **obligation/shame/guilt spiral** that you felt paralyzed. Weak. Willing to spend twenty precious minutes being passive-aggressively harangued over your religious beliefs (or lack of them) to avoid what you perceive as an even more difficult confrontation.

Wouldn't it feel good to just say what you mean and mean what you say? Just…do unto others as you would have them do unto you? I mean, it's right there in the Bible.

# Vote no on giving a fuck!

Here I'm going to offer a personal story to illustrate just how much I believe in the NotSorry Method and how it has worked for me. Names have been changed to protect the identities of certain family members, but the circumstances are, I assure you, 100 percent real. Those involved might read this book someday and recognize themselves, but they need feel no shame. NotSorry is about living your best life — and they don't want to be on the other end of *my* political grandstanding any more than I do on theirs.

Unlike an election, everybody wins!

One evening, my husband and I were enjoying a lovely dinner with two family members when the topic of our nation's then-president — and the veracity and completeness of his birth certificate — surfaced over a plate of delicious fried seafood. Allegations were leveled, opinions were expressed, and before it could turn into a long-form debate, I looked each family member right in the eye and said, "Dick, Jane, I love you, but we are not having this conversation." Then I turned to my husband — who shares my political views but who wants to talk about them an awful lot more than I think is necessary — and said, "I mean it."

There wasn't even a hint of hurt feelings. We changed the subject, had some laughs, licked the last of the tartar sauce from our fingers, and trundled off into the night.

THAT is how a family dinner should be. And it can be, if you budget your fucks accordingly.

---

### But what if it all ends in tears???

What I've been trying to get across by drilling my method into you and emphasizing the importance of being honest *and* polite is that when NotSorry is practiced in good faith, tears are statistically unlikely to occur. There's always a chance things could go badly, sure, but there's a much greater chance that you could be entering into a whole new phase of decreased conflict and mutual respect among your family members.

And if your family is full of hysterical crybabies, then do you really want them to keep inviting you over?

---

# Refuse to play the shame game

**Shame is lonely and isolating,** and guilt is a direct result of shame. I offer my research results in order to show that **you are not alone.** Plenty of other random strangers from all over the world took my survey and proved that they share one another's lack of fucks on any number of hot-button family issues.

Which means it's entirely possible that several members of your own family get just as riled up as you do when Uncle Jim uses the Christmas ham as his personal soapbox or Cousin Renée forces kabbalah bracelets on all of the guests at your rehearsal dinner.

**And if you're not alone, then you don't need to feel so much *shame* over your decision to not give a fuck.**

There is safety in numbers. By harnessing the power of consensus, you will feel better equipped to decide when you well and truly don't give a fuck, and to proceed with confidence.

# Holidays: A personal policy

My husband and I have a policy with regard to Thanksgiving, and it's served us very well. Please feel free to steal or amend it for your own benefit:

We have three sets of family to see in any given year. Unlike Orphan Black, we can't be in three places at once. AND WE DO NOT WANT TO PLAY FAVORITES. So about eight or nine years ago, we told our families that we were starting a three-year rotation and that henceforth, we'd be doing the holiday with each group in a prescribed order, no exceptions. Nobody gets to double up because *this year* Aunt Marie has a big birthday or because the cousins got a great deal on an eight-person cruise (and they need us to make the head count), or because somebody has a new girlfriend we need to meet. Talk to me if she's still around next time we get to your year. I even skipped my fifteenth high-school reunion because it took place during my in-laws' Thanksgiving year (not that I particularly gave a fuck about the reunion, but that's beside the point). Rigid? Sure, but **nobody's feelings get hurt, and that is truly something to be thankful for.**

Well, well, well. The finish line is in sight!

We've almost reached the end of our Four Categories of Potential Fuck-Giving, and if I've done my job, you're already

| **Five more things people don't give a fuck about when it comes to family** |
| --- |
| 1. Keeping up with group texts |
| 2. "Stories told to me by my parents about people I grew up with, which I already know from Facebook" |
| 3. "Hiding my drinking from them when they are the reason I drink" |
| 4. "The goddamn hypercritical piling on" |
| 5. "My parents' dogs, whom they refer to, inexplicably, as their 'granddogs'" |

reaping some life-changing magic. At the very least, you've been introduced to some new tools and strategies for getting what you want out of life, and you feel validated knowing there are other people out there just like you who want (or don't want) those same things.

But before we close the book on Family, there's one more subcategory that begs to be addressed. It cajoles. It pressures. It *demands* attention. You know what (who) I'm talking about.

# In-laws

Remember what I said about choice? Well, unless you are born into a culture that enforces arranged marriage, you do get to choose your spouse, but you do *not* get to choose your in-laws. If that's what marriage was about, we'd be a one-night-stand economy.

**Yes, by getting married, you've essentially doubled your family fuck-giving in one fell swoop.** It's sort of like when you get a bonus at work, and you're like, "Awesome!" and then the IRS proceeds to tax it at 50 percent, and you're like, "WTF?"

Your in-laws are basically a package deal; what you really wanted to ride home off the lot was your spouse, but the dealership threw in some extra people for free. Some of them could wind up being nice perks, like those armrests in the backseat with built-in cup holders; others...maybe not so much.

But as with your own family, which you did not choose to be born into, it is perfectly acceptable to parcel out your fucks to your in-laws according to what minimizes your annoy (and maximizes your joy) while treating everyone in a respectful way.

It certainly helps if you and your spouse can get on the same page with regard to your collective fucks, and if you can agree to **divide and conquer.**

For example, if a member of your family is getting married, having a baby, turning a year older, or celebrating any milestone that typically encourages gift-giving, the household time and energy allocated toward acquiring that gift should probably fall on your shoulders. And if the gift is meant for someone on your spouse's side of Ancestry.com, he or she should handle it. (May I suggest simply gifting everyone a copy of this book?)

There's no way around it; there are going to be many daily (or semiannual) line items added to your Fuck Budget when you inherit a bunch of new family members. But if you think about it — **they inherited you too.** And *your* religious values, and *your* political views, and *your* holiday traditions, and *your* aversion to dressing in matching turtlenecks for group photos.

**When it comes to not giving a fuck, you might have more in common than you realize!**

Therefore, by practicing the NotSorry Method as it

pertains to your in-laws, you can ignite a chain reaction that culminates in an increase of happiness and harmony — and a decrease of fucks given — for all involved.

# The homestretch

This is the last time you'll have to venture inside your mental barn, and the Family fucks you've been storing in there are probably buried three-deep under a blanket of cobwebs and resentment. You have my sympathy. Like holiday decorations, Family fucks take up valuable space even in the middle of June — but once you dust 'em off and haul those fuckers out into the light, most of your work is done.

So make that final list, and make it count!

# FAMILY* STUFF I MAY OR MAY NOT
# GIVE A FUCK ABOUT
### (*Including In-Laws)

_____    _____

_____    _____

_____    _____

_____    _____

_____    _____

_____    _____

_____    _____

_____    _____

_____    _____

_____    _____

_____    _____

_____    _____

_____    _____

_____    _____

# Consolidating your lists

And there you have it! By now, you've acquired the tools for deciding whether or not you give a fuck and sorted all your potential fucks into manageable categories. You've waltzed around your mental barn and shone your metaphorical flashlight into its darkest corners, illuminating the fucks you've been collecting in there since ... well, since before you read this book.

Step 1 of the NotSorry Method — deciding what you don't give a fuck about — is well within your grasp.

You should have four exhaustive lists of things you may or may not give a fuck about from each of your four categories. (And a numbness in your lower extremities.) The good news is, now we can get to the fun part — crossing things off!

**Remember as you go that "giving a fuck" is akin to spending your time, energy, and/or money on anything that made it onto one of your lists. By crossing something out and NOT giving that fuck, you should GAIN more time, energy, and/or money to spend on everything else.**

First, you need a giant black marker. Because there is nothing more satisfying than crossing things out with a giant black marker. Some might even call it a "magic" marker...

Sorry, couldn't resist.

Then, as you sit on the floor for the final time among

your inventory lists — the physical manifestation of your mental barn–decluttering tour — take note of which fucks evoke those feelings of joy or annoy in your heart, your head, and your gut.

An agreeable fluttering in the chest or groin? Joy! Let your magic marker pass over these items like the Angel of Death passed over the firstborn sons of Israel.

Palpitations, dread, nausea? All of these are criteria for crossing off a fuck or three.

Finally, in *her* book, Marie Kondo advises thanking each object — a dress, a handbag, etc. — for its service before discarding it. But I'm not so sure the items on your no-fucks list deserve thanks, are you? They've drained your time, energy, and money for too long.

No, what I want you to do is this:

As your black marker hovers over those that annoy, touches down, and inscribes decisive strokes through the fucks you're about to stop giving, you should **utter a quiet, ceremonial "Fuck you" to each and every one.**

Feels good, doesn't it?

Now you're almost ready to take Step 2 and then start amassing magical, life-changing rewards! I'm delighted at how far you've come in such a short time. But hey, juuuuuust to make sure we're on the same page here, what about the things you *didn't* cross off your list?

Sure you don't want to rethink any of those?

# Do not underestimate the drain of infrequent fuck-giving

There may be some things that are still sitting there because you thought, *Eh, it's not like this comes up very often. Probably easier to just give the fuck and not deal with the fallout.*

Have I taught you nothing?

Maybe I wasn't clear enough—and for that I accept full responsibility—so let's just go over the concept of the Broken Windows theory one more time. **If you continue to give your fucks willy-nilly to things that annoy, those fucks will continue to be expected of you.** Like useless paperwork and *Keeping Up with the Kardashians* reruns, this is a vicious cycle.

Remember how a personal policy sets a precedent, in a positive way? Giving a fuck also sets a precedent—and makes it exponentially harder to stop giving that fuck in the future.

If you have already committed to doing the time-consuming work of sorting your fucks into categories and making your lists and drawing up your Fuck Budgets, then why take the easy way out and continue to spend your fuck bucks on things that annoy, just because they only come around once or twice a year?

By that logic, you will never achieve enlightenment. But you will spend every Christmas hungover and caroling in ten-degree weather wearing a stupid sweater.

# Giving a fuck

Finally, if you've consulted the flowchart on page 39, worked your steps, and determined that there are indeed things on your lists that you give a fuck about, then go ahead, give them! Giving a fuck is easy. You don't need me for that. (Though I thank you for your patronage.)

**For everything else, it's time to put Step 2 of the NotSorry Method — not giving a fuck — into action.**

# ⦀

# Not giving a fuck

You are on the cusp of not giving a fuck. The view from up here is pretty special, isn't it?

In part II, you learned to qualify the fucks you give based on whether they annoy or bring joy. You quantified them based on whether they fit into your Fuck Budget. And you've been introduced to the tools and perspective — namely, feelings, opinions, honesty, and politeness — with which to make those calculations.

You sat down on the floor and you made all those lists and you decided which fucks you just don't give. Maybe you even had to buy a new black marker because your first one ran out of ink. (I've seen it happen.) I congratulate you; really, I do.

But it's about to get so much better.

Because in part III...you will actually STOP GIVING A FUCK.

Excited? Yeah!

Nervous? Don't worry; I was too.

Let's start by visualizing everything you stand to gain. This ought to get you psyched up and ready to give no fucks like the champ you are.

# The holy fucking trinity: Time, energy, and money

Time, energy, and money are the things you gain by ceasing to give a fuck. And it's extremely useful to **keep them foremost in your mind when gearing up to take Step 2.** Visualizing your gains releases endorphins into your brain. And in my professional opinion, endorphins are magic.

**So take a minute and think about all the joy Step 2 will bring.** For example:

## Time

Sometimes all you want is a free hour to take a leisurely bath and clip your toenails. By not giving a fuck about making an appearance at your neighbor's vegan BBQ, you get back that hour. Soak it in!

## Energy

Sometimes you wish you could get up and go to the gym at six in the morning when no one else is watching. By not giving a fuck about attending someone's ill-conceived ten o'clock Tuesday-night dinner party (WTF?), you can stay sober, rest up, and be bright-eyed and bushy-tailed on Wednesday for your date with the elliptical machine.

## Money

Sometimes you want that Caribbean vacation so bad you get sand in your shorts just thinking about it. By not giving a fuck about your grade-school friend's wedding that you don't understand why you were invited to in the first place, you can march on over to JetBlue.com and reallocate the thousand dollars you totally would have spent on it before reading this book, and you can do it with a clear conscience. NotSorry all the way to the Virgin Islands, baby!

Another way to visualize your gains is to take the items on your no-fucks list and plug them into the Venn diagram below. This way, you can clearly see where your time, energy, and money is being spent, and what you can get back by not giving those fucks.

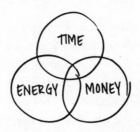

**With this in mind, let's revisit your lists.**

Mark a little *T* next to all the fucks that, when not given, result in more *time* for you to spend as you wish. Then do an *E* for *energy*, and, finally, an *M* for *money*. (It might be hard to see them through the line from your giant black marker, but I have a feeling they're pretty fresh in your mind.)

Some items will fall in just one segment of the diagram, some in various combinations of *T* + *E* or *E* + *M*, etc. And, obviously, it's not giving the fucks situated smack in the middle of where *T* + *E* + *M* intersect that will free you up in the most delightful ways possible.

Unfortunately that also means they're probably going to require the most attention paid to other people's feelings and opinions, communing closely with your Fuck Budget, potentially developing some personal policies, and making a few tough calls with regard to being an asshole.

But we can work with that.

My eventual diagram with regard to the Ten Things About Which I, Personally, Do Not Give a Fuck list on page 52 looks like this:

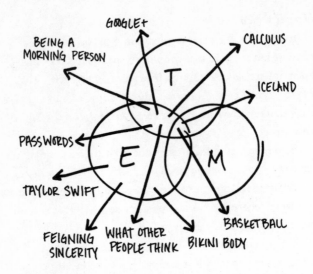

As you can see, mine is heavy on time and energy concerns, less heavy on money.

This makes sense because in my view, time is a finite resource, energy is somewhat renewable under the right circumstances, and there's always more money to be made (plus: credit cards).

And to those of you who just choked on your minimum-wage paycheck, please understand that what I'm saying is that for *me,* compared to time — which started running out literally the second I took my first breath — additional money can at least *potentially* be earned or borrowed if need be; there is no such thing as "borrowed time." Although I'm sure if American Express could figure that one out at 16.9 percent interest, they would.

But different strokes for different folks! **It doesn't really matter *which* resources are more valuable to you when doing this exercise, just that you learn to recognize them.** Whatever the permutations of your diagram, looking at the items that fall within the categories that are most valuable to you will stand you in good stead when it comes to taking Step 2.

And help you start taking back that time, energy, and money!

Oh, hey, did you hear that? Those are your endorphins talking. They told me to tell you you're doing great.

# Baby steps

Not giving a fuck can be as simple as hanging up on a telemarketer, calling in sick on your birthday, or throwing on a baseball cap to meet the plumber at 7:00 a.m. instead of getting up two hours early to shower and blow-dry your hair like you're entering *Maxim*'s Hometown Hotties contest.

But no matter how revved up you get by making your lists and deciding to do away with a passel of fucks, when push comes to shove, **Step 2 can often take a little wind out of your sails.** In order to avoid getting stalled on the open water with only a ham radio and a smile, I recommend diving (figuratively) back into the method that got you here.

By that I mean, start very deliberately with the fucks on your list that affect only you. This way, you can get comfortable with taking Step 2 before you ever have to confront other people's feelings (which, as you may know, can be *supremely* inconvenient).

You might not even need to be polite. In fact, all you really have to be is honest — with yourself.

# Threat level yellow: Easy fucks to stop giving

**Don't give a fuck about your Facebook friend's constant drama?** "Unfollow" is one of the easiest ways to not give a fuck ever invented. None of the confrontation of "Unfriend" and all of the benefits. Thank you, Mark Zuckerberg!

**Don't give a fuck about wrinkles?** Stop spending money on lotions and serums, time applying them to your face, and energy worrying about the visible signs of aging, which — spoiler alert — are actually impossible to counteract unless your name is Christie Brinkley. Hot damn, she looks good.

**Don't give a fuck about understanding the stock market?** Stop banging your head against the *Wall Street Journal* just to make yourself sound knowledgeable at dinner parties. (And maybe get yourself a financial adviser — the good ones pay for themselves.) Instead, use that time to become an expert on something that is truly meaningful to you — perhaps small-batch bourbon? — and let someone else field all the stock tips for your friend group.

# Threat level orange: Medium-tough fucks to stop giving

This is when you move on to fucks that are clearly **unreasonable drains** on your time, energy, or wallet. The stuff that — while it may affect other people or require a conversation about opinions and/or feelings — is still, objectively, not your problem.

**Don't give a fuck that your forty-year-old friend has to move apartments tomorrow and is asking for helpers "in exchange for beer"?** Pure honesty ("I can't be responsible for your failings as an adult") may not be the best policy here, but you can still politely beg off, citing some vague work commitment. After all, what does he know about work commitments?

**Don't give a fuck about promoting synergy in the workplace?** At first you might worry that your boss is going to call you out on this one, but rest assured, *synergy* is exceedingly difficult to quantify and your lack of fucks won't change that. Reserve this creative energy for something that will benefit YOU — like devising the winning bracket in the office NCAA pool.

**Don't give a fuck about your coworker's decision to procreate?** It's as easy as not putting any money in that Diapers.com gift-card envelope they're passing around the office. Worried that people will think you're cheap? **Please revisit page 25.**

# Threat level red: The hardest fucks to stop giving

These are the fucks that are going to require all your tools plus a fair amount of self-possession and maybe a personal policy or two. **They involve other people, have high potential for hurting feelings/being an asshole, and are often socially unacceptable.** In other words, what the NotSorry Method was invented for. Time to gird those loins!

**Don't give a fuck about extended-family weddings, graduations, and similar events?** These things are usually planned fairly far in advance. That's how they get you. I recommend a visualization exercise: Before you blithely check the "Yes" box on the RSVP card, making a dent in your Fuck Budget before the reality of the consequences can sink in, think about how you're likely to feel *on that day* — or, worse, the night before, when you're in line at airport security on your way to third cousin Barry's *Star Wars*–themed wedding in Pittsburgh. As Yoda might say,

"In a dark place we find ourselves, and a little more knowledge lights our way." If you can access that deep reservoir of despair *before* you RSVP, you're going to save yourself days (weeks? months?) of regret and anxiety leading up to the event *and* thousands of dollars in airfare and hotels. Simply check "RSVP Regrets" on the response card and send a gift. Perhaps a nice Death Star cutting board?*

**Don't give a fuck about your friends' children?** First, you need to make it clear that it's not just *their* children — it's all children! In that way, it's somewhat of a personal policy. (And if you're a parent yourself, "all children except mine" works too.) However, literally saying the words "I do not give a fuck about your children" is unlikely to yield positive results. You may never have to deal with those kids again, but you've also probably lost a friend. Assuming you do NOT want to be expected to attend functions where the guest of honor is a toddler, or ever, *under any circumstances,* be asked to babysit — but you do want to keep your friends — then you have to add a heaping helping of politeness in with that honesty. An occasional lollipop or *So cute!* shout-out on social media can be very effective. It's the whole "spoonful of sugar helps the medicine go down" philosophy. (Mary Poppins: NotSorry since 1934.)

**Don't give a fuck about puppies?** Yeah, good luck with that.

---

* http://www.thinkgeek.com/product/iovg/.

# A pep talk

I should acknowledge right here, right now, that even after you've made your decisions about which fucks not to give, and you've diagrammed your lists and started with the easy stuff, it's not always going to be smooth sailing. Obviously people like myself and Richard Simmons have it all figured out, but if not giving a fuck was that easy, you'd all be doing it already.

**Yes, you heard it here first: You may be tempted to backslide a little.** It's common. No worries. Like the birth control pill, the NotSorry Method is revolutionary but not 100 percent foolproof. If you find yourself experiencing early-morning nausea, just try to keep in mind this cautionary tale.

## The party no one wants to go to

**Recall that coworker's karaoke birthday party we talked about in part II**. Let's say you've decided — in making your category lists — that you truly don't give a fuck about karaoke, or Tim, or maybe about birthday parties in general. In fact, you're quite sure that almost no one in your office wants to go to this party, but now that you're reading this book, you're the only one feeling brave enough to say no. You implement Step 2 and skip the party.

Success!

But then the next day, you feel somewhat uncomfortable. Maybe Tim or others are giving you the cold shoulder. (Focus: Do you give a fuck about what they think?) You falter. You begin to question your decision not to have given a fuck about your coworker and his party. You spend a few more energy fuck bucks just worrying about it.

Stop right there.

**It is important not to confuse this unfamiliar feeling of freedom with feelings of regret or shame.** You made the right decision. For God's sake, they sang an *entire* Kenny Chesney album! That's not a twinge of regret* you are experiencing; that's freedom with a side of pity for the rest of your coworkers.

About most of whose opinions you will, eventually, stop giving a fuck.


# Honesty: A sliding scale

I spent a lot of time in parts I and II hitting you over the head with the two keys to taking Step 2 without being an asshole: honesty and politeness. And although I do allow that in some instances, being polite is overrated (see page 96,

---

\* If you truly feel you are experiencing regret, it's time to add Regret to the list of things you don't give a fuck about.

"Sometimes It's Okay to Hurt People's Feelings"), honesty is actually the more, shall we say, *flexible* of the two principles.

**Honesty is *usually* the best policy when not giving a fuck.** It tends to level the playing field and helps you avoid a lot of that exhausting bush-beating-around — not to mention the "social media handicap" when you've been dishonest about why you can't be somewhere and then you have to worry about being spotted on Facebook or Foursquare (is Foursquare still a thing?) "checking in" or "earning a badge" at some rival event.

So many extra fucks given!

Coming at your fucks from an honest perspective allows you to say things like "I'm sorry, I don't have time to read your self-published novel about gnomes, but I wish you all the best with it" or "I don't like tea." Simple and direct and, if delivered politely, very effective.

**Not hurting people's feelings *and* not getting caught in a lie is the purest form of NotSorry. You have nothing to agonize over or apologize for.**

But we all know there are times when you've taken Step 1 and decided not to give a fuck, and you've charted your most polite and honest course of action, yet implementing Step 2 feels...icky. The good news is, if you're feeling that "ick" factor, it means you're not an asshole. They never get the jitters.

My point is, if you have a hunch that full-blown honesty is NOT, in fact, the best policy, you can fudge it a little. For reference, I've compiled a handy list:

## Times when full-blown honesty is perhaps not the best policy

When it involves someone else's cooking

When it could just as easily be "a matter of scheduling"

When you don't want to have to talk to anyone's therapist about it

When Santa and small children are part of the equation

When dealing with a pregnant woman

When dealing with your mother-in-law

When dealing with your pregnant mother-in-law

# Different fucks, same principle

In part II, we worked on **deciding** what you don't give a fuck about. Then, earlier in part III, we reviewed some concepts to get you psyched up. **Now — using real responses from real people as prompts — we will tackle NOT GIVING THOSE FUCKS.**

That's right, in this section, I'm returning to my research!

Using the results of my anonymous survey, I will provide you with examples of things that crop up regularly on other people's No-Fucks-Given lists and show you how one might go about not giving fucks to those items without — say it with me — *becoming an asshole.*

**To ease you into your practice of NotSorry, I've provided three levels of Step 2–taking,** depending on your personality type and how comfortable you are being "no-nonsense" about this nonsense.

## Let's start with Category One: Things

At the time of this writing, more than 10 percent of responders singled out the Kardashians or a specific member of the Kardashian family (I'm looking at you, Kimberly) as something they don't give a fuck about, with another 10 percent responding *reality TV, reality-TV stars,* or *people famous for being famous.* I don't know what to tell you guys — this problem is bigger than all of us. I've spent a little time pondering the existential question *If so many people don't give a fuck about the Kardashians, then why are they all over my television set?* but I quickly concluded: *I don't give a fuck.*

Moving on.

Beyond the reality-TV gang — including bachelor/ -ettes, housewives of wherever, and Duggars — a few other celebrities cropped up in the Things I Don't Give a Fuck About category, among them Madonna, Hugh Jackman, and Drake. I think it's pretty easy to proceed with Step 2 and not give a fuck here (unless you're Drake's mom, I guess), so I'm going to address some more pressing matters:

**Recycling.** The NotSorry Method is all about prioritizing your happiness and preserving your time and energy for things you care about. So if you don't care about saving our planet…

> **Beginner:** Resolve to recycle bottles and cans, but stop worrying about whether wax-coated paper and Styrofoam are eligible. Shhh…I won't tell.

> **Intermediate:** By all means, put that fleet of empties in the regular trash instead of bothering with separate bags and cans. You partied hard last night. You need a rest.

> **Expert:** Delegate the recycling to your spouse or roommates and give it not another fuck. Plausible deniability. Look it up.

**NPR.** I personally have nothing against NPR—Hi, guys! Feel free to book me on any one of your many illuminating, entertaining programs!—but I do understand the impulse to not give a fuck about something the rest of society seems to fetishize, especially when it's served up with a healthy dose of elitism. (See my views on the *New Yorker*, page 56.)

**Beginner:** When someone mentions NPR, say, "Wait, wait, don't tell me," and then walk away. They'll just assume you're being clever.

**Intermediate:** Make up a fake NPR show, tell people it's your favorite, and enjoy watching them pretend like they listen to it too.

**Expert:** If you've successfully stopped giving a fuck what other people think, then the next time your friends start waxing poetic about *All Things Considered,* you can hold your head high and pronounce those five liberating little words: "I don't listen to NPR."

**N.B. rosé.** See above, but substitute the words "I don't like rosé" and then enjoy watching everyone at the table secretly think, *Neither do I. What am I doing with my life?*

**Who "really" wrote Shakespeare's plays.** If you're a Shakespeare scholar, you have to give a fuck about this, or at least pretend to. Everyone else? Not so much.

**Beginner:** When someone at a cocktail party presses the Christopher Marlowe argument, mutter, "A Marlovian, eh?" and then spit on the ground. He'll get the message.

**Intermediate:** If you get cornered, make like Hotspur in *Henry IV, Part One.* Say, " 'O gentlemen, the time of life is short!'" Then swoop off into the next room and quickly pull an Irish good-bye.* (Excellent, *excellent* strategy for not giving a fuck under innumerable circumstances, by the way.)

**Expert:** Don't go to these parties in the first place.

*Game of Thrones.* Another fairly simple execution of NotSorry, as no one is forcing you at sword point to read the books or watch the show (though that would be kind of awesome in an ironic way). But in terms of having to *listen* to other people talk about reading the books and watching the show, you still need to be prepared.

**Beginner:** "Oh…you're still talking about this? Sorry, I zoned out. Guess I won't get invited over to watch the finale—darn!"

**Intermediate:** An honest, polite "Hey, guys, since I don't really give a fuck about *Game of Thrones,* I'm gonna duck out now and catch up with you Tuesday morning when you're

> ### My favorite survey response
>
> DRESSAGE: I had to look this up, and when I got to the part of the Wikipedia entry that says, "Dressage is commonly referred to as 'horse ballet,'" I added it to my Things I Don't Give a Fuck About list as well.
>
> Thank you for expanding my horizons, whoever you are.

---

* An Irish good-bye is when you leave a party or gathering without telling anyone. Highly recommended.

done hypothesizing about what really happened to Jon Snow and how it's different from the books."

**Expert:** Invest in a T-shirt that says

**Dragons Don't Give A F*🐎*ck**.
Wear it every Monday as needed.

**Social media.** Where to begin? In our modern world, not being on Facebook is akin to being a Communist in 1950s Hollywood. Lemmings don't like it when other lemmings don't fall in line. I myself am the proud owner/operator of Facebook, Twitter, and Instagram accounts (though, as you know, I draw the line at Google Plus). But if you're one of the happy few committed to a "Like"-free life, stay strong. There are no hashtags where you're going.

> **Beginner:** Maybe just pick one platform, set up a shell page, and forget about it. Facebook privacy settings are a bitch, so I recommend lurking on Twitter — that's where all the good stuff is anyway. People behave very, very badly on Twitter.

> **Intermediate:** Fine, don't open any accounts, but also don't *talk* about how you have no Facebook page. You're just asking for trouble.

> **Expert:** Have you heard of "Catfishing"?

**Who anyone else is attracted to.** Kudos to you, Enlightened One! If you know this is something about which you give no fucks, it is extremely easy to proceed to Step 2.

> **Beginner:** See those two people of the same sex over there nibbling each other's ears? Isn't that cute?

> **Intermediate:** Flipping through a magazine, you spy Billy Joel's fourth wife and her skin that glows like moonstone in contrast to his sexy, sexy gin blossoms. Turn the page.

> **Expert:** It is *so monumentally easy* to not give a fuck about who anyone else is attracted to, that once you reach expert level you owe it to your fellow citizens to *not only* not give a fuck, but to remind all the people you encounter in the act of giving this fuck how idiotic they are for doing it.

---

**Fitting in.** This — THIS RIGHT HERE — is why I wrote the book you are holding in your hands. Whether you are a beginner, intermediate, or expert no-fuck-giver, *The Life-Changing Magic of Not Giving a Fuck* is for people who are exhausted by presenting a façade of interest, enthusiasm, and conformity to the rest of the world. It is about empowering them (you) to feel free to be themselves (yourselves) and live their (your) best lives.

---

# Category Two: Work

Many, many people who took the survey responded that they don't give a fuck about meetings, conference calls, and dress codes — items we already covered in depth in part II. But here are some additional common refrains that are obviously in dire need of the NotSorry treatment:

**Unsolicited e-mail, answering of.** This is a good example of something that *technically* affects someone else (i.e., the sender of the e-mail) besides you, but if the original message was unsolicited, it doesn't count.

> **Beginner:** You are hereby authorized to not give a fuck. Hit Delete and spend a little extra time surfing Gawker. God knows *they* don't give a fuck.

> **Intermediate:** Delete the e-mails *and* block the senders. That'll teach 'em.

> **Expert:** Run one of those fancy Unsubscribe programs for your entire in-box full of e-newsletters, coupon codes, and Kickstarter updates. The effect is not unlike taking your first hit of heroin (or so I'm told).

**Gossip.** If you really don't want to be a cog in the office rumor mill, there are a variety of ways you can handle it with a minimum of fucks given.

**Beginner:** Close your door, if you have one. If not, invest in a pair of headphones. What's the point of gossiping with someone wearing headphones? Exactly.

**Intermediate:** A polite "I don't want to hear it" and then casually covering your ears with both hands until they walk away should get your point across nicely.

**Expert:** Next time someone mentions your coworker Regina's sexting habit, simply put up your hand and repeat after me: "Imma tell her you said that." Voilà! You are no longer trusted with gossip.

**Team-building exercises.** It's bad enough that we all have to work together day in and day out; do we really have to work on our *working*? It's like starring in a bad Fellini movie but with worse coffee.

**Beginner:** Take a vacation day.

**Intermediate:** Take a sick day.

**Expert:** Take a personal day.

**Kissing ass.** In part II, I said that for every one thing you *have* to give a fuck about at work, there must be five that you don't. Kissing ass is one of them. Do your job well and there should be no need to debase yourself by brown-nosing the boss, his assistant, or the woman in Public Relations with whom the boss is rumored to be having an affair.

**Beginner:** Just don't do it. It's easy to opt out of something that's not even part of your actual job description.

**Intermediate:** If ass-kissing is demanded by the aforementioned boss, consider snapping a photo of him and his paramour and engaging in petty blackmail instead. Same fucks expended, more satisfying result.

**Expert:** Employ reverse psychology. If there are some aspects of your job you really *should* give a fuck about but don't, then ass-kissing might actually come in handy. It's your world, squirrel.

**Coworkers' kids.** When Paul from Accounting starts yapping away about his daughter's fifth-runner-up finish in the local spelling bee, you may think you have no recourse. But you would be wrong.

**Beginner:** Clutch your stomach and say, "Hey, that's great, but I've got to run!" Honest and polite — and for all Paul knows, you're suffering from crippling diarrhea (an excellent spelling-bee word, BTW).

**Intermediate:** "Huh. Weird. I wonder where she got that from?" Honest, borderline polite, this is what we in the business call a "mic drop."

**Expert:** "Oh, that's nice. *My* daughter is illiterate." Paul will never speak to you again. About anything.

**The company mission statement.** Have you heard of the Infinite Monkey theorem? They used it on an episode of *The Simpsons* where Mr. Burns has a thousand monkeys typing at a thousand typewriters, the idea being that if given enough time, the monkeys could produce the works of Dickens. This is essentially how company mission statements are created, and why you need not give a fuck about memorizing or adhering to them. They are the products of untold man-hours of "brainstorming" and "focus-grouping" resulting in the blandest, most generalized, least-potentially-offensive, frequently asinine copy that could have been created by any group of monkeys in any boardroom in America.

> **ALL LEVELS:** I suggest that every time you encounter a corporate mission statement, rather than reading/absorbing it, you instead spend two minutes imagining a roomful of monkeys smoking cigars and happily click-clacking away. I honestly think that would be more useful to you.

**"Whose job it is."** This is a double-edged sword. Clearly none of us *want* to be doing other people's jobs. But I hear ya loud and clear on not giving a fuck about "whose job it is" when that argument becomes an excuse to not complete some perfectly simple task that is otherwise holding up the entire project. Charlene in Intimates isn't restocking her panties in a timely fashion and nobody else wants to pitch in? Fine, she sucks, but none of us can get out of here until the whole Ladies' Department is spic-and-span.

> **Beginner:** Just do it yourself and take it up with management on Monday. You may expend some time and energy, but you'll have fun getting Charlene fired next week. Net gain.

> **Intermediate:** Do her job this one time (and plan to report her), but just for kicks, leave a note from the Thong Fairy advising Charlene that her days are numbered.

> **Expert:** Suggest that everyone draw straws to see who has to bat cleanup. Keep a trick straw in your pocket at all times.

**Other people's weekends, the full rundown.** It may come as a shock to some of your coworkers, but weekends are where most people go to avoid "work, doing of" and "coworkers, talking to." Upon your arrival back at the office on Monday, if you find yourself confronted with a coworker's Tale of Stand-Up-Paddleboarding Lessons on Martha's Vineyard, you can always implement the same Step 2 strategy you used with Paul and his spelling prodigy.

As Bert Lance, director of the Office of Management and Budget in Jimmy Carter's 1977 administration, once said, "If it ain't broke, don't fix it."

**Beginner:** "Gotta run!" [*Clutches stomach.*]

**Intermediate:** "Um...thanks for the visual?"

**Expert:** "My [wife/husband/significant other] died in a freak paddleboarding accident."

**Performance evaluations.** You probably have to show up to your performance evaluation if you want to keep your job. But—and I know this may sound counterintuitive—you don't have to give a fuck about it while you're sitting there. Why? Because this is a situation in which the die has been cast. That evaluation has already been rendered by your boss; today just happens to be the day you have to *listen* to it.

**Beginner:** Picture your boss in his underwear. Hopefully this will relax you, not gross you out.

**Intermediate:** Picture your boss in a gimp suit and sequined heels.

**Expert:** *Wear* a gimp suit and sequined heels to your performance evaluation and immediately become the mayor of No Fucks Given.

**How much of a "true fan" of Tarantino your coworker is.**
Only one person submitted this response, but I hope that
whoever you are, you're reading this book because this is,
like, the Holy Grail of not giving a fuck. I hope your
coworker is reading it too, because he or she deserves to be
Step 2'd all over the place. Just lay it down. Be totally
honest. You don't even need to be polite. Please, put
yourself and everyone else at your office out of your
collective misery.

---

### The ultimate no-fucks-given to work: Quitting your job

Getting this far into *The Life-Changing Magic of Not Giving a Fuck*
may mean confronting some difficult truths about your job.
Namely, that you hate everything about it. You took the barn
tour, made your lists, and realized that your mental filing cabinet
is bursting with annoy. The doors won't close no matter how
hard you shove, and you're increasingly worried the whole thing
is going to fall down on top of you and crush you to death.

If that's the case, I hate to break it to you, but not giving a
fuck about conference calls and coworkers' kids isn't going to be
enough. You need a new job entirely. We're talking *Ultimate Step
2: Quitting*. Fine, maybe you can't quit TODAY — I'm not saying
you should put down this book, set fire to the tassels on your
boss's Gucci loafers, and blaze out with no thought to where your
next paycheck will come from.

But think about it this way: You're *already giving a fuck* about
your paycheck every day. So the act of looking for a new one
might cost you a few short-term time and energy fucks, but

---

they're in service to long-term joy! Once you're installed in the new gig, you'll be back down to a single fuck given in pursuit of a single paycheck. When you get there, maybe treat yourself to a new filing cabinet. You've earned it.

## Category Three: Friends, acquaintances, and strangers

I'm going to take a slightly different tack here, because the circumstances under which you might not give a fuck about items and events related to friends, acquaintances, and strangers are **more fluid, numerous, and complex than in any other category.**

And also because variety is the spice of life.

Unless you change jobs (and sometimes even then), Work has a relatively finite fuck list (same you-know-what, different day), Things are largely inanimate and therefore require less finesse when it comes to taking Step 2, and Family maintains a fairly stable rotating cast of fucks year after year (thanks in part to those delightful holiday traditions we discussed earlier).

But friends, acquaintances, and strangers are, on the whole, less predictable. They come in and out of your life with more regularity (especially strangers, who are constantly popping up with their petitions and their terrible parking jobs and their "community-outreach meetings"), and they often move in packs that can make it difficult to navigate through Step 1, let alone execute Step 2.

Luckily, there's one universal life event that — if you can even come close to mastering its labyrinthine twists and challenges — will provide a blueprint for nearly all interactions in this category.

Sort of a case study, if you will.

# You wondered when we'd get to weddings, didn't you?

I like weddings. Weddings are fun and joyous celebrations of love. I have had an absolute blast at about forty-two of them in my lifetime. So when the inevitable Amazon reviewer quotes this next part out of context, just remember that all I'm saying is what everyone knows to be true: weddings make a huge dent in your Fuck Budget.

Remember that Venn diagram? Weddings sit squarely at the intersection of time, energy, and money.

The first few you go to are novel experiences. There's dancing, booze, free cake, maybe a photo booth. Woo-hoo, weddings! As time goes on — especially for readers in their twenties and thirties who have similarly aged friends and siblings and cousins — you'll probably go to lots more. They will become a little less novel and, by virtue of their frequency, possibly a little less fun, or at least more of a drain on your time and energy. Certainly a lot more expensive. And suddenly you've got twelve wedding invitations — plus related events like engagement parties and bridal showers and bachelor/-ette parties — and only so much disposable income and so many vacation days in a year.

If you're in your fifties, sixties, and seventies, now you're getting invited to your friends' kids' weddings! Which means you have even less of a stake in the party but it takes just as much time, energy, and money to get there.

**There's no shame in admitting that not every person's wedding until the end of time is a wedding that you, once invited, must attend.**

You often make sacrifices to be part of your friends' (or friends' kids') special days and you're happy about it. But sometimes? Sometimes you may not be able to afford their destination of choice. You may want to go to the wedding but not be able to fit sixteen related events into your calendar. You may not actually know these people very well. Or you may just not want to or not be able to go for one or more of a host of reasons that are perfectly justifiable.

We've all been there, even if I'm the only one willing to admit it in print. Other people's weddings are where the Enlightened go to knock back warm shots of well vodka and beg for mercy in the arms of a willing bridesmaid.

# Old fucks, new fucks, borrowed fucks, blue fucks

The reason that weddings provide such a helpful case study in the grand scheme of Category Three fuck-giving is that **they involve friends, acquaintances, and even total strangers, ALL AT ONCE.**

Think of it this way: Your wedding, your fucks. Add in-laws, and you've got your hands full. But when it comes to *someone else's* wedding, you still wind up being asked to give a fuck about all kinds of things, each of which is likely tied to a friend or family member of your friend and so on and so forth, which means many of those people are mere acquaintances or strangers to you.

For a brief (or not so brief) period, you're inheriting enough fucks to power a small nation's GDP. Tuvalu's, say, for an intimate ceremony. Or the Federated States of Micronesia's for a big black-tie affair.

**Don't give a fuck about contributing a photo to the slide show for the rehearsal dinner?** That's your prerogative — but it affects your friend, who WILL notice the conspicuous absence of your third-grade Laverne and Shirley Halloween costumes, plus it affects whatever poor sap was roped into organizing the slide show to begin with and who has to collect enough pics to fill a PowerPoint the length of "My Heart Will Go On." (Fuck PowerPoint.)

It also probably affects the mother of the bride, because everything affects the mother of the bride.

**Don't give a fuck about deciphering the dress code of your pal's "Semi-Formal Creative Summer Cocktail Casual" wedding at the groom's DC country club in the dead of August?** Sure, you can wear your no-fucks-given Old Navy romper, but then you run the risk of (a) horrifying the in-laws, (b) ruining at *least* two pictures, and (c) making everyone else at the reception extremely jealous about how comfortable you are. Possibly so jealous that someone "accidentally" spills Shiraz on your romper.

When it comes to weddings, Step 2 should be taken very, very carefully to achieve maximum NotSorry and minimum sobbing brides, terminated friendships, and credit card debt. We're talking "hazmat-suit" levels of care taken. (Come to think of it, it's really too bad hazmat suits are not appropriate wedding attire.)

But once you've mastered the delicate dance of honesty and politeness required to navigate a wedding with minimum fucks given, you're on your way to getting the most possible joy — and the least amount of annoy — out of not only every wedding you do (or do not) attend, **but out of life in general.**

That's right, applying the NotSorry Method to other people's weddings is a master class in and of itself!

Up ahead, I've detailed four common wedding-related

scenarios in which you might someday find yourself wanting to give no, or fewer, fucks. They will test your resolve, challenge your adherence to the method, and nudge you ever farther down the path of enlightenment. Each is accompanied by an **Honesty and Politeness Matrix**, with the points on the matrices denoting the relative honesty/politeness of your action so you can see precisely where your stated goal of not giving a fuck aligns with peak NotSorry practice — and when you're dangerously close to (or situated deep inside) the Asshole Quadrant.

## The wedding that takes place over a holiday weekend

**The situation:** Your friends are getting married during a long weekend that you traditionally reserve for a fun vacation or annual family gathering. Maybe a national holiday is the only time the bride and groom can get off from work. Or maybe they're teachers, so spring break is their jam. Maybe they hope that people will be glad to have the extra day off work to put toward attending their wedding — and that's very nice of them, really! — but now you have to choose between allocating your fucks to the Vacation You Look Forward to All Year Long and Three Days of Salmon and Small Talk in Tampa. Your goal is to proceed with the former.

**How do you respond?**

# THE WEDDING THAT TAKES PLACE OVER A HOLIDAY WEEKEND

HONEST

"WE USUALLY GO TO MIAMI WITH FRIENDS OVER LABOR DAY. MAYBE WE COULD BRING THEM TO YOUR WEDDING INSTEAD? LMK!"

RSVP A SIMPLE NO AND SEND A NICE GIFT.

"I'M HONORED TO BE INVITED BUT UNFORTUNATELY CAN'T MAKE IT."

IMPOLITE

"WOULD YOU CONSIDER CHANGING TO ANOTHER WEEKEND?"

POLITE

"AW, THAT'S OUR TIME-SHARE WEEKEND IN MAUI. I WISH I COULD DO BOTH!"

"I'D LOVE TO COME, BUT I JUST SCHEDULED AN APPENDECTOMY... IN THE HAMPTONS."

ASSHOLE QUADRANT

DISHONEST

## The destination bachelor or bachelorette party

**The situation:** You and your significant other are already spending hundreds (thousands?) of dollars plus precious vacation days to travel to your friends' wedding. But yay, it's their special day! However, the bachelor and bachelorette parties are also taking place a flight-and-a-hotel away from your home. Call it Vegas and Montreal, respectively. If these are your best friends in the world and you want to move heaven and earth (and your Visa card) to make it happen, go right ahead. Those are the fucks you want to give! But for the purposes of this matrix, we're assuming that you can't afford the combination of time, energy, and/or money, and you don't want to go — but you also don't want to look like an asshole.

**How do you respond?**

# THE DESTINATION BACHELOR OR BACHELORETTE PARTY

**HONEST**

"SOUNDS AWESOME! I'D TOTALLY GO IF SOMEONE ELSE WAS PAYING!"

"THANKS SO MUCH FOR THE INVITATION, BUT I JUST CAN'T AFFORD IT."

RSVP WITH REGRETS, BUT SEND A BOTTLE OF CHAMPAGNE / A STRIPPER TO THE HOTELS.

**IMPOLITE**

**POLITE**

"THE DESERT AIR IS REALLY BAD FOR MY SINUSES, PLUS I DON'T WANT TO GO."

"I'M ACTUALLY NOT ALLOWED IN CANADA ANYMORE."

ASSHOLE QUADRANT

**DISHONEST**

# The wedding with six thousand activities

**The situation:** Your friend's fiancée is SUPER-active. She and her family just can't sit still or everyone would have to start confronting their *feelings*. Thus the wedding-weekend invitation comes with an additional pamphlet of activities, like morning yoga, kayaking, a nature hike, charades, and a bride's side vs. groom's side croquet tournament. All of these things would, for you, mar an otherwise idyllic (and fucking expensive!) weekend at the fancy spa retreat where the wedding is being held. You want to book a massage and a round of golf, not suffer through an 8:00 a.m. scavenger hunt with a bunch of perky strangers.

**How do you handle it?**

# THE WEDDING WITH
# SIX THOUSAND "ACTIVITIES"

**HONEST**

BEG OFF THE ACTIVITIES
BECAUSE YOU WANT TO
BE "WELL RESTED" FOR
THE MAIN EVENT!

**IMPOLITE** ← → **POLITE**

SIGN UP FOR A COUPLE
THINGS TO KEEP UP
APPEARANCES BUT PLAN
ON GETTING FOOD POISONING.

MAKE IT A POINT TO
TELL THE BRIDE HOW
"SPECTACULAR" THE
NATURE HIKE WAS...
EVEN THOUGH YOU
DIDN'T GO.

"PAMPHLET?
WHAT PAMPHLET?"

SAY THE ACTIVITIES LOOK
SO FUN BUT YOUR DOCTOR
ADVISED YOU TO "TAKE
IT EASY UNTIL YOUR
STITCHES COME OUT."

ASSHOLE QUADRANT

**DISHONEST**

# The morning-after brunch

**The scenario:** Many weddings come equipped with brunches to round out the weekend; these typically take place before hotel checkout time, and at least half the wedding guests have massive hangovers. You intend to be one of those guests and you want as much time as possible to sleep it off before catching your $480 flight home. You also don't want to face any of the relatives you might have scandalized the night before with your Rihanna-made-me-do-it dance routine, and you especially don't want to do so over dry toast and an egg buffet.

**What do you do?**

# THE MORNING-AFTER BRUNCH

**HONEST**

- RSVP NO, BUT INSTEAD OF CHECKING THE "NO" BOX, CROSS IT OUT AND WRITE "FUCK BRUNCH."

- RSVP YES* WITH AN ASTERISK (*IF IT'S AN OPEN BAR!!!)

DON'T RSVP, BECAUSE YOU <u>MIGHT</u> SHOW UP, AND YOU THINK IT'S BETTER TO EXCEED EXPECTATIONS

RSVP NO WITH A LITTLE SAD FACE NEXT TO IT.

**IMPOLITE** ← → **POLITE**

RSVP YES KNOWING THAT YOU HAVE NO INTENTION OF SHOWING UP, AND BLAME IT ON A "MIGRAINE."

ASSHOLE QUADRANT

RSVP NO BECAUSE "THE ONLY FLIGHT OUT IS AT SEVEN" AND IF CAUGHT CHECKING OUT AT 11:59 A.M., SAY IT WAS DELAYED.

**DISHONEST**

I hope and trust that this has been a useful exercise. The Honesty and Politeness Matrices are designed to show that **the NotSorry Method is simple, but not inflexible.** It can work for different people in different ways, depending on the circumstances.

Just don't wind up in the Asshole Quadrant, and you'll be all set!

# Getting cold feet? Revisit your personal policies

When it comes to weddings or just life in general, if the no-fucks list is long and your capacity for honesty and politeness is wearing thin, don't forget that instituting a new personal policy for friends, acquaintances, and strangers is always an option. Of course, you don't want to overuse this tactic or people will start to catch on. Think of it as a football coach calling for an onside kick — you want it to be surprising and impossible to defend. If done right, it can be a total game-changer.

## Category Four: Family

As discussed in part II, so many of the survey responses overlapped when it came to Family that we've pretty much covered the gamut already, with perhaps one glaring omission.

In fact, when it comes to this response, glaring omissions are part of the problem. That's right, I'm talking about **INHERITANCE.**

No surprise, as this one sits at the nexus of the tools and actions we've studied in both Step 1 (affects other people, feelings/opinions, overall Fuck Budget, obligation/guilt) and Step 2 (honesty and politeness, being/not being an asshole).

Whether we're talking cash or heirlooms, the issue of inheritance seems to result in an inordinate number of fucks given in the form of time and energy spent haggling and complaining over who gets/deserves what, or who didn't want/deserve what in the first place.

**And yet, many survey respondents claim they don't give a fuck about money/inheritance when it comes to Family.**

*Hmm.*

I can only assume that since money is universally acknowledged as one of the most difficult/taboo topics in any relationship, even those who decide they don't give a fuck about splitting Grandpa's stamp collection among six siblings — and who are willing to cop to it in an anonymous survey — can have a hard time going full NotSorry with their families.

Inheritance can be a thorny issue, no doubt about it. But if all of the people who professed to not give a fuck about matters of inheritance **actually did not give those fucks** — loudly, clearly, and unequivocally — then we could all spend our time enjoying the family and Inverted Swan stamps we have before we have to start mourning the ones we don't.

Deep, I know.

# Performance bonuses!

In part II, I acknowledged that **when it comes to Family, some fucks are nonnegotiable, but I said I'd show you how to make the most out of a less-than-ideal situation.** So if you've completed Step 1 and decided what you don't give a fuck about, but you know that taking Step 2 (not giving that fuck) is just completely impossible, no way, José, literally not over your mother's dead body, then you might as well, in the act of giving that precious fuck, **build in some performance bonuses.**

For example, if you just can't avoid a family holiday get-together, schedule a massage for the day after so you have something to look forward to. Even better, request the massage as your holiday gift so your family is essentially paying you back for the fuck you gave!

(#ProTip: Upgrading to first class on the flight home is also an effective, if wildly expensive, balm for the enervating family gathering.)

Or if you have to sit through your mother's Rotary luncheon at which she's being honored for outstanding service to the community that you grew up in and fled immediately upon turning eighteen, steal one of the honoree's Percocets from the medicine cabinet beforehand.

And if you can't realistically opt out of the group photo, resolve to wear your kinkiest or most hilarious undergarments that day and I guarantee you the whole process will be more bearable. Plus, when the pic starts clogging your Facebook feed with comments like *Beautiful family!!!!* and *OMG they're so grown up!* you will take secret pleasure in knowing you were wearing your POISON PARTIED HERE thong.*

# FUQs (Frequently Uttered Questions)

Oh, like you've never made a bad pun before. Go ahead, judge me. I don't give a fuck; it's my book!

Aaaaanyway, I thought it might be helpful to address a few of the most common questions I receive when I talk to people about the NotSorry Method — questions that I'm pretty sure are popping into your head even as you gleefully cross items off of your various lists. I know how it is,

---

* I may or may not be the proud owner of a POISON PARTIED HERE thong.

believe me. You've made some big decisions, but *actually* not giving a fuck? That's easier fantasized about in the comfort of your own mind than said out loud at Shabbat dinner. My advice is to harness the fever while it's burning hot within you. No time like the present to get your fucks in order and start living your best life!

**On that note, here are some FUQs to help you feel better about taking Step 2.**

Q: **Telling people I don't give a fuck feels awfully impolite in and of itself. Don't you think it's kind of rude?**

A: Well, if the F-word gives you pause, you don't actually have to say it out loud. You can communicate your decision to not spend your time, energy, or money on something in a totally G-rated fashion (e.g., "I confess I don't share your opinion on X, but you do you!"). I don't think it's as much fun, but that's for me to give a fuck about, not you.

Q: **I'm worried that if I stop giving a fuck about too many things, I'm going to like it so much that I become a lazy sack of shit with nothing and nobody to live for.**

A: It's a legitimate concern, but the goal of the NotSorry Method is *not* actually to get to #ZeroFucks (an amusing if impractical hashtag). It's to pare away the fucks that don't bring you joy, *paving* the way for the fucks that do.

**Q:** **If not giving a fuck is supposed to be so liberating, why does it feel so uncomfortable?**

**A:** Not wearing clothes is liberating too. But it can also be uncomfortable because society isn't ready for this jelly. All it takes is a little confidence (and a little baby powder); you'll see.

**Q:** **How am I supposed to explain all of this to my mother?**

**A:** Just mail her a copy of this book. That's how I plan to handle it.

**Q:** **Even though everything you've said makes perfect sense [Why, thank you!], I just know I'm not going to get away with giving fewer fucks when it comes to _____.**

**A:** All I can say is, you won't know until you try. Remember I told you that my husband thought I was completely out of my gourd when I asked him if I could tidy up his sock drawer? And look how that turned out!

**Q:** **What if I decide I don't give a fuck about something, and then I don't give the fuck, and then I regret it?**

**A:** Now you're just stalling.

**Q:** **I wouldn't want people to tell me they didn't give a fuck about something that was important to *me*, so how can**

**I tell them I don't give a fuck about something that's important to *them*?**

A: Let me throw it back at you in a different way. Would you want people to feel obligated and/or guilted into doing something for you that you *knew* they didn't want to do? The answer to THAT question should always be no, or you're an asshole. And you wouldn't know that they felt this way unless they were comfortable telling you, and vice versa. This is precisely how taking Step 2 unlocks life-changing magic for everyone.

# Getting more from the fucks you do (or don't) give

Once again I want to revisit the overarching goal of the NotSorry Method, which is not merely to stop giving fucks to things that annoy—it's to free ourselves up to give better, higher-quality fucks to things that bring joy.

If part III of this book was all about not giving those fucks, then get ready to bask in the second half of the equation: gaining more time, energy, and/or money for everything else.

**Which brings us to part IV, where, as they say, the life-changing magic happens...**

## IV

The magic of not giving
a fuck dramatically
transforms your life

By this point in your study of NotSorry, you've stopped giving a fuck about what other people think, developed excellent fuck-allocation skills, and created a robust list (and handy reference guide) of things you don't give a fuck about, plus a manageable list of things you absolutely, 100 percent *do* give a fuck about.

Bravo!

Chances are, you've reclaimed hundreds of hours that you used to spend on those people and things you didn't give a fuck about, and, if you've done it properly, you haven't been fired and Gail from Marketing hasn't burned your house down. You've sorted out your feelings about obligation, pub trivia, and Iceland. You've lost only those friends you didn't really like anyway, and you've avoided making new ones you don't need. Not only that, but you've probably become an even more honest, more polite person than you were when you started out—which is an excellent by-product, if I do say so myself.

You're moving ever closer to that enlightened state of essential fuck-giving that I mentioned in part I. By putting your fucks in order, casting out those that annoy, and identifying the people and things that bring you the most pleasure and satisfaction, you're living your best life.

Speaking of which, part IV even contains a list of fucks you probably should—and could—be giving now that you have all this time, energy, and money on your hands.

Fucks that could open up a whole new landscape of joy!

If you still need more convincing, please, by all means, keep reading...

# A fuck not given is something gained

In part III, I recommended that you **envision your potential gains** in order to make taking Step 2 a little easier. And assuming you went through with it — hurray! — it's worth it now to **quantify exactly what you *have* gained.** I think you'll find it quite satisfying and more than a little motivating.

As mentioned, the first thing people tend to get back when they put their fucks in order is TIME. Time to meditate quietly on the toilet instead of rushing to get on a conference call; time to cultivate that prizewinning fudge recipe on a Sunday afternoon instead of reading *Moby-Dick* for your book club (who picked that?); time to spend with a loved one instead of, well, time to spend with some random fuckers you don't even like.

So what have you gained thus far in terms of time? Three hours? Ten minutes? One weekend a month? I smell a list coming on!

## TIME I HAVE GAINED BY NOT GIVING A FUCK

| ACTIVITY | BENEFIT |
|---|---|
| Example: Not watching the VMAs | 2 hours |
| _____ | _____ |
| _____ | _____ |
| _____ | _____ |

The second thing the NotSorry Method returns to you is ENERGY. That can be as simple as taking a blessed nap or as complex as conserving energy by not doing one activity — that CrossFit class you only signed up for because your friend pressured you into it — and then *expending* it on something you'd rather be doing, like finally cleaning out your car because it's starting to smell like you imagine that lady from *Goonies* does.

## ENERGY I HAVE GAINED BY NOT GIVING A FUCK

ACTIVITY

BENEFIT

Example: Not getting wasted
at Margarita Monday
with coworkers

The will to live on
Tuesday

_____        _____

_____        _____

_____        _____

_____        _____

Last but not least is MONEY. As the American humorist
and performer Will Rogers once said, "Too many people
spend money they haven't earned to buy things they don't
want to impress people that they don't like." Sing it, sister!

And because money is so easily quantified, it is
especially satisfying when you apply the NotSorry Method
and it results in tangible financial gains. If you stopped
giving a fuck about, say, designer clothes — in part because
you've stopped giving a fuck about what other people
think — you could stand to save hundreds or thousands of
dollars in any given year. I know so many women, especially
in cosmopolitan New York City, who feel pressured to fit in
by way of overspending on name-brand labels when clothes
at half the price would look good and make them perfectly
happy.

Or say you're a suburbanite who stopped giving a fuck about traveling every Sunday to your six-year-old nephew's soccer games — let's just say he's unlikely to go pro and snag you free tickets to the 2034 World Cup. Not only are you saving time and energy, you're saving gas money! That $2.50 a gallon really adds up, and Auntie needs a new pair of off-brand sunglasses.

## MONEY I HAVE GAINED BY NOT GIVING A FUCK

| ACTIVITY | BENEFIT |
|---|---|
| Example: Not going to that Vegas bachelor party | $1,000* |
| _____ | _____ |
| _____ | _____ |
| _____ | _____ |
| _____ | _____ |

---

* Occasionally you have to spend *some* money to be a good friend and gain peace of mind. In this case you might want to send a singing telegram, so the formula is $ SAVED ($1,000) – COMPENSATORY $ SPENT ($200 on singing telegram) = NET SAVINGS ($800). Still not bad!

**Yes, the path to enlightenment is paved with reclaimed hours, newfound verve, and cold hard cash.**

# Your fucks affect your body, mind, and soul

But there's more! What you may *not* have anticipated gaining from the simple act of not giving a fuck is an **overall improvement to your physical and emotional health.**

Think about it: You haven't gained merely time, energy, and money — you've gained self-knowledge, confidence, and a childlike zest for life. Plus, you've saved yourself a lot of headaches. Literally. Not to mention heartburn, anxiety, and nausea. Remember that coworker karaoke party you skipped out on? Think of the hangover you could have had! You'd have been guzzling 'ritas all night just to keep from strangling Tim from IT with his own mic cord. The next morning would have been brutal, trust me.

But no fucks given? No fitful night's sleep, no headache, no dry mouth during your morning presentation, no silently counting the minutes till you can take a covert nap under your desk at lunch, no crick in your neck from taking said nap . . . I mean, the rewards shown in the cost-benefit analysis here are undeniable.

You have more **time** to do what you really want to do after work (sit on the couch in your underwear eating Pop Tarts and watching *Ultimate Ninja Warrior*);

You have **decided** that watching *Ninja Warrior* is more pleasurable for you than singing karaoke with Tim from IT (and you have acted on that knowledge **because you no**

**longer give a fuck what Tim or anyone else thinks** about your priorities);

You have more **energy** in the morning to put toward the **necessary fuck-giving** of shaving without hurting yourself (face, legs, or bikini line — hungover shaving is not to be trifled with);

And you have the **money** you'd have spent on tequila plus the late-night Domino's order with which you would have attempted (inadequately) to soak up all that alcohol.

Yes, you'll be whistling Dixie in the break room while your coworkers are taking uncomfortable naps under *their* desks. You'll probably get a lot more done that day too, because they'll be too hungover to bother you!

**Consider the further exciting benefits to your body, mind, and soul that can be derived from simply not giving a fuck:**

## Body

So many extraneous fucks lead to hangovers — we've discussed that in depth — but what about the ones that lead to actual physical injury?

I vividly remember a morning when I spent an extra ten minutes playing Words with Friends against my brother instead of leaving to catch my train. I knew I was cutting it close, but it made me so happy to totally *annihilate* him with ZAX on a triple word score before heading to the office.

Of course, when I made my way down to the platform, I saw the train about to pull out of the station. I ran (in heels —

before I stopped giving a fuck about those) to catch it and missed it by inches, twisting an ankle in the process. I was sweaty and panting, rapidly swelling, and extremely pissed off.

As a result, I added "running to catch trains" to my list of Things I Don't Give a Fuck About, and I've since saved myself a fortune in orthopedic work.

## Mind

Mental decluttering is even better than physical decluttering because it doesn't stop at the bounds of a ceiling or wall. The inside of your skull may still be filled with squishy gray matter, but those intangible planes of anxiety, worry, panic, and fear have been swept cleaner than a church before the pope's visit. The mental-health benefits of not giving a fuck are vast and never-ending.

For example, just think what might happen, decades from now, if *today* you decide to stop giving a fuck about sitting through Sunday church services (Sorry, Pope) and instead dedicate that fuck to completing the Sunday *Times* crossword puzzle every week. Future you, not suffering from Alzheimer's, is hugely appreciative! You just can't buy that kind of peace of mind.

## Soul

It's about to get a little woo-woo here, but bear with me for a moment. Although not everyone puts stock in the traditional definition of the soul as some ethereal life force separate from our physical beings, I'd wager that most of us understand the concepts of "soul-crushing" or "soul-destroying" as they pertain to things that hurt us on a deep, cellular level. Not things that just crowd our calendars or sap our strength, but the kinds of activities or tasks or people that, we feel, place grave limitations on our very freedom. Yes, I realize I sound like Mel Gibson in *Braveheart* here.

Well, I contend that *freedom* is another word for *soul* and that by not giving a fuck to all the wrong things, and conserving your fucks for the ones that make you happy, you stand to gain the kind of freedom that some people might even describe as…dare I say…"soul-affirming."

## Another way to give no fucks

The NotSorry Method is largely concerned with the active giving or not giving of fucks. Even when you've decided not to give a fuck, Step 2 often requires some *action* on your part—declining an invitation, saying no to a meeting, explaining your latest personal policy. And then there are fucks you may decide to give *instead,* which consume time, energy, and money—albeit of the sort you're happy to spend.

But there's another way to not give a fuck that is actually quite passive and similarly transformative in both the short and long term. I equate this version of not giving a fuck to mentally repeating the phrase *It's just not worth it.*

You may find it useful to pursue this technique when, for example, someone on the other side of a necessary transaction — such as a boss or a cable company — is being a real asshole or supremely incompetent but there's nothing you can do about it. I mean, you could explode, causing high blood pressure, risking your job, and/or getting your cable connection mysteriously taken offline. But that's not productive when all you want to do is clock out, go home, and watch ESPN2 in peace.

In cases like these it's easy to fall victim to righteous indignation, a state that itself burns up more fucks than your smarmy/moronic adversary is worth. Rather than letting that bad juju consume you like a lady praying mantis consumes her lover after sex, just try... not giving a fuck.

Say to yourself, *It's just not worth it,* and move on.

# Paying it forward

By becoming one of the enlightened few who roam the earth giving no fucks, you will inevitably wind up conferring your newfound wisdom on your fellow man. I can't tell you how many people have listened to me rave about the effects of my NotSorry Method and resolved, right then and there, to make changes of their own. I've helped coworkers see the light when it comes to useless paperwork, helped friends make better decisions regarding the use of their vacation days, and even aided my own parents in giving fewer fucks. They're so proud.

I'm not doing all of this to be altruistic, either. I don't give a fuck about altruism! I do it because it makes ME feel good—let me tell you, if not giving a fuck feels great, helping someone else stop giving a fuck feels that much better.

And finally, I do it because if all of us gave fewer fucks and were exponentially happier and healthier, the world would be a better place. For me.

# Knowing what you can do without

Also known as "what you probably never had to give a fuck about in the first place."

A terrific side benefit of learning not to give a fuck is that as you accept the consequences or "growing pains" of the first few attempts, you gradually get into a rhythm where you stop second-guessing yourself—which significantly reduces time spent giving a fuck, as well as concomitant anxiety levels. **Hesitation (and anxiety) spells extraneous fucks every time.**

In this way, the NotSorry Method gives you the tools and perspective to approach life from a different point of view, that of someone who can quickly and easily evaluate any situation and act accordingly. And it allows you to devote that regained time (and energy, and money) to other things.

Here's the best part: **You'll find that not giving a fuck about some things does NOT necessarily result, over time, in an *equal replacement* of fucks given to other things.**

You'll probably discover that once you stop giving a bunch of fucks to things that don't make you happy — and start adding back in some neglected items that do — **you don't even really need quite so many things in your life to begin with.** That there *aren't* forty-seven previously ignored tasks, events, people, and pursuits that merit replacing the forty-seven of which you've finally divested yourself.

I don't know about you, but for me, it's simply not possible to completely fill twenty-four hours every day with things I give a fuck about.

In other words, I have a lot of downtime, and it's fucking great.


# Things about which you should probably be giving more fucks

Full disclosure: It's about to get a little counterintuitive up in this piece. Don't say I didn't warn you. (Because I did warn you, on page 172.)

Until now we've focused mainly on a one-to-one ratio

of fucks given/not given—like leaving work at five o'clock sharp in order to catch the first inning of the Dodgers game or forgoing your friend's *Survivor: Monkeys vs. Robots* finale party so you can eat a bag of Tostitos and finish reading this book. Those are legitimate, in many cases even daily, rewards. And they will change your life.

But once you've gotten the hang of the NotSorry Method, you might find yourself willing, able, and even excited to take it all a step further. **The magic, you see, can work on an even grander scale.**

I'm sure you've seen those lists that go around social media every so often with titles like "Twenty Pieces of Advice for Twenty-Year-Olds from a Retiree" or "What People on Their Deathbeds Regret Most in Life"—and maybe you thought, *Whatever, I have another few decades to go before I have to worry about any of that.*

As Javier Bardem in *No Country for Old Men* might say, "Think again, friendo."

The reality is, unless we've been given a ballpark figure by a reputable physician (and sometimes not even then), not a single one of us knows when we're going to shuffle off this mortal coil. It's morbid, but it's true. Tomorrow you could get hit by a bus, or mauled by a pack of wolves, or be scared to death by a clown.

**When you think about it like that, don't you want to make every second count?**

Sometimes that means giving some new, *prolonged,* fucks in lieu of all the piecemeal fucks we've tackled thus far.

In order to help you do that (because that's just the kind of gal I am), I took the liberty of scouring the Internet for myriad versions of the lists mentioned above, and cherry-picked five of the most commonly referenced regrets — aka **Things About Which You Should Probably Be Giving More Fucks.** Bear in mind that these are not to be confused with the actual short-term gains you might have already realized as a result of adopting the NotSorry Method. No, these are **long-term goals,** the fulfillment of which can easily and irretrievably be lost to the day-to-day fuck-giving that dominates most people's lives.

In no particular order, here they are:

## Traveling

A trip here and there as a reward for not giving a fuck about some other obligation is one thing, but what the people who contribute these lists to the annals of the Internet are talking about is true traveling. Wanderlust. Going global. Traveling could become a regular part of your life, not just a semiannual boys' weekend in Tahoe (although those are nice too).

## Taking better care of your health

Frankly, exercise for the sake of burning calories and sweating through my sports bra is not something I give a fuck about, but health isn't just about how many squat thrusts you can do. Health is also about overarching goals like sleeping more, staying calm, and maybe also not shotgunning a whole cheese pizza á la Liz Lemon in times of stress. Which has been more than a once-in-a-while proposition for me, I don't know about you.

## Learning another language

Rome was not built in a day, nor was conversational Italian mastered in the one hour you saved by skipping that infernal team-building workshop. But even if you have absolutely zero desire to read Dante in the original, it's worth noting that this regret looks like plenty of others — running a marathon, say, or growing your own vegetables — that are terrifyingly easy to put off because *c'è sempre domani.*

## Planning for retirement

Maybe you don't give a fuck about having a stable, sustainable income when you're too old and decrepit to show up at an office every day. Maybe your working theory is "Live hard, retire in penury." That's cool, but it seems like a *lot* of sixty-somethings feel otherwise, so I'm just putting it out there.

## Mastering an awesome party trick

If you're the kind of enlightened individual who has successfully reduced your Work, Friends, and Family obligations enough to spend a few hours a week blissing out and juggling flaming bowling pins for no other reason than because you fucking feel like it, you officially win at life.

# You do you

But maybe you're a homebody. Maybe you're already an exercise nut. Or maybe, like me, you're woefully uncoordinated and will never learn to juggle. The point is, you don't *have* to give your fucks to anything on the above list, or to anything else that ANYONE else gives their fucks to.

**You can take or leave my suggestions.**

*The Life-Changing Magic of Not Giving a Fuck* is meant to be aspirational and inspirational — not tyrannical — in its teaching. My stance on karaoke, for example, is likely to be unpopular with at least half of the people reading this book. It may also be puzzling to those who have seen me perform "Faith" or "Like a Virgin" while under the twin influences of rum punch and peer pressure. Whatever. I do me, you do you!

In writing this book, I heard from not only hundreds of

anonymous strangers who responded to my survey but also from my friends and family, my literary agent and her assistant, my editor and publicist and others at the publishing house, and a few strangers who happened to be in the right place at the right time. (You're welcome.) From these conversations, I realized that everyone's path to enlightenment is paved by a unique combination of fucks given and not given, and that one person's joy can easily be another person's annoy.

**And that's okay. Your fucks are *yours*— to value and prioritize and give as you see fit.**

You're also allowed to change your mind, revise your personal policies, and reallocate accordingly. You've heard of a crime of opportunity? Well, sometimes you might commit a fuck of opportunity, and that's par for the course. I mean, I really, truly don't give a fuck about karaoke, but if I'm already at the bar and someone dangles that microphone in my face and I'm lubed up with enough Bacardi to anesthetize a pony, well…things happen.

What I'm saying is, in the heat of the moment, you might find yourself giving an unexpected fuck and it might even bring you joy. Or at least bring the people watching you make a fool of yourself some joy, which isn't the worst thing you can do for your fellow man every once in a while.

# Fuck the haters

In the vein of that very first admonition I handed down re: not giving a fuck about what other people think, I wanted to pay special attention to a subset of those people, aka the haters. At this point in your study of the NotSorry Method, you're likely to encounter a few of them, and you need to be prepared. These people are, at the least, baffled, and at the most, grievously offended by your life decisions. For whatever reason, they just don't have the desire or wherewithal to accept NotSorry into their lives. And that's okay! But you don't have to be weighed down by their narrow-mindedness or insecurity. Your life is great and getting better every day. Fuck the haters.

# On achieving enlightenment

No matter where you stood on the NotSorry spectrum when you started this book, I trust that you've made progress in your own personal quest to give fewer fucks and join the ranks of the Enlightened, among whom are myself, Serena Williams, and New York City news anchor Pat Kiernan.* Seriously, that guy has parlayed not giving a fuck

---

\* https://en.wikipedia.org/wiki/Pat_Kiernan.

into an *art form* — we should all aspire to be more like Pat Kiernan, who stars as himself in *The Amazing Spider-Man 2* and the new *Ghostbusters*.

But back to you. You've come this far, so you must have wanted it at least a little bit, right? You must have been fed up with looking at your life as a series of obligations to be met, people to tolerate, and calendar squares to be desperately reshuffled until a blessed wild card in the form of a free afternoon rose to the top.

Or maybe this book was a gift from a friend, in which case he or she might be trying to tell you something.

Whatever the path that brought you here, I hope that *The Life-Changing Magic of Not Giving a Fuck* has shown you that all of this is possible, and without your having a nervous breakdown. Two weeks in rehab can be nice and all, but you needn't get to the end of your rope only to hang yourself with it.

Wow, that got dark…sorry.

What I meant was, the NotSorry Method is not only practically prescriptive, it's also prophylactic! It can cut you down from the rafters, but what's more, it can keep you from ever climbing up there in the first place. You may wish to refer to it daily, as one might a holy Bible, or periodically, like a public-transit map. You can treat it like a GPS for your soul. Or you can take it out into a field and shoot it. It matters not to me.

*Really, Sarah, why is that?*

**I think you know why.**

# Afterword

In the time since I started writing *The Life-Changing Magic of Not Giving a Fuck,* I've seen a lot of people giving a lot of fucks they didn't want or need to give. I've witnessed friends working through the weekend for no additional compensation, people agreeing to dates they have no desire to go on, and my own husband fighting a losing battle with a call-center employee. It buoys my spirit to know that the NotSorry Method is now available to all these folks in their time of need, a core philosophy to aid them in living their best lives from here on out.

In 1837, Hans Christian Andersen wrote a fairy tale called "The Emperor's New Clothes" in which a delusional monarch parades through town naked while under the impression that he's wearing a suit so fine that it is invisible to anyone who is "hopelessly stupid" — or so the con artists who sold him the suit led him to believe. The emperor himself can't see it, but of course he'd never admit that. Nor would his many advisers, who wish to keep their jobs. And the townspeople along the parade route not only pretend to see the garments, they offer praise for the beauty of the fabric and the fineness of the tailoring. Until, that is, one child calls out, "But he isn't wearing anything at all!" Finally, the crowds, liberated by the truth, admit that they can see what's been in front of them all along.

I like to think of myself as that child. Except the emperor is society and his clothes are time-, energy-, and money-wasting burdens on my life, and I'm standing here shouting, "I don't give a fuck!"

And you, the townspeople, don't have to either.

This is my dream.

And although even I have yet to achieve NotSorry nirvana, I am traveling farther down the path of enlightenment every day. For instance, just this week I gave fewer fucks to Thai food, late-night television (I will miss you, Jon Stewart!), and the Democratic National Committee than I ever have. Stop calling me, guys. It's really annoying.

Finally, I've spent a lot of time justifying the concept of not giving a fuck to people who think it sounds…a little bitchy. Kind of mean. Borderline sociopathic, maybe?

That's too bad. On one hand, I don't want them to think poorly of me. But on the other hand, I'm out here giving fewer, better fucks and living my best life.

And guess what?

I'm not sorry.

# STOP
# GIVING
# A
# FUCK

# AND START LIVING YOUR BEST LIFE!

# Acknowledgments

I feel lucky to live in an age where the no-fucks-given antics of public figures, as well as the occasional common man, are broadcast far and wide. In no particular order, I would like to thank these members of the Not Giving a Fuck Hall of Fame* for inspiring me every day as I wrote this book:

## The Not Giving a Fuck Hall of Fame

**October 3, 1992**: Sinéad O'Connor rips up a picture of the pope on *Saturday Night Live*.

**January 20, 2015**: Ruth Bader Ginsburg falls asleep at the State of the Union...because she was drunk.

---

* Got Hall of Fame submissions of your own? Send them to magicofnotgaf@gmail.com. I love reader mail!

**July 25, 1965**: Dylan goes electric.

**September 13, 2009**: "Imma let you finish" at the 2009 MTV Video Music Awards, feat. Kanye West.

**February 28, 2011**: Charlie Sheen appears on the *Today* show, demands $3 million per episode of *Two and a Half Men,* and claims to have "tiger blood" DNA.

**June 7, 1993**: Prince changes his name to an unpronounceable symbol in order to breach his contract with Warner Brothers.

**December 15, 2011**: RIP Christopher Hitchens, giver of no fucks.

**March 10, 2003**: Natalie Maines tells an audience in London that the Dixie Chicks "are ashamed that the president of the United States is from Texas."

**October 19, 2015**: Passenger allegedly strangles a woman on Southwest Airlines for leaning her seat-back on him.*

**February 16, 2007**: Britney Spears shaves her head, gets tattooed, and one week later attacks a car with an umbrella.

---

* http://gawker.com/man-allegedly-strangles-woman-over-reclining -seat-1737308260.

**October 21, 1992:** Madonna publishes a coffee-table book of erotic photos called *Sex,* which features her then boyfriend…Vanilla Ice.

**September 21, 2015:** Pizza Rat doesn't give a *fuck.** 

My husband, Judd Harris, gives the vast majority of his fucks to me on a daily basis. Not only that, he's been coaching me to live my best life since 1999. He is the fucking best.

My agent, Jennifer Joel, is the epitome of sophistication and class, so her seal of approval on this project meant a lot to me. Her support has been complete and unwavering from the get-go. She's a fucking star.

My editor, Michael Szczerban, saved me from myself on any number of pages and did so on the tightest of deadlines and with great aplomb. He is both a brilliant editor and a really fucking good guy.

Many folks at Little, Brown and ICM — including but not limited to Ben Allen, Reagan Arthur, Sabrina Callahan, Meghan Deans, Nicole Dewey, Liz Farrell, Lauren Harms, Sarah Haugen, Andy LeCount, Charles McCrory, Garrett McGrath, Madeleine Osborn, Miriam Parker, Tracy Roe, Cheryl Smith, and Tracy Williams — gave their fucks

---

* https://www.youtube.com/watch?v=UPXUG8q4jKU.

liberally to all aspects of this book's publication. Jane Sturrock at Quercus UK, Frederika Van Traa of Kosmos in Holland, Mariana Rolier from Rocco in Brazil, and Ulrike von Stenglin from Ullstein Verlag in Germany led the international charge. Go, Team NGAF!

My parents didn't flinch at the title. My grandmother, however, was told I was writing a book about ducks.

Finally, *The Life-Changing Magic of Not Giving a Fuck* wouldn't have been so comprehensive without the contributions of hundreds of people all over the world who responded to my anonymous survey and who shall therefore remain anonymous. There were also a few dozen friends and family members who offered inspiration along the way, and who would probably *prefer* to remain anonymous. I can respect that.

Once you read the book, you'll know who you are — and know that I thank you.

# Index

# About the author

GEORGE TOWNLEY

Sarah Knight lives in Brooklyn (when it's warm in New York) and the Dominican Republic (when it's not) with her husband and their ill-behaved cat, Doug. In 2015, she quit her corporate job to go freelance — a move that enabled her to give fewer fucks to winter, meetings, and conference calls, and many more fucks to sunshine and mojitos. An editor, writer, and cum laude graduate of Harvard University ('00), where she was also the first-ever female president of the Hasty Pudding Theatricals, she expects the speaking invitations to start pouring in from her alma mater any day now. Learn more at sarahknightbooks.com or follow her on Twitter and Instagram @MCSnugz.